ECSTASY

UNDERSTANDING THE PSYCHOLOGY OF JOY

ALSO BY ROBERT A. JOHNSON

He: Understanding Masculine Psychology
She: Understanding Feminine Psychology
We: Understanding the Psychology of Romantic Love
*Inner Work: Using Dreams and Active Imagination for
Personal Growth*

ECSTASY

UNDERSTANDING THE PSYCHOLOGY OF JOY

Robert A. Johnson

HarperSanFrancisco

A Division of HarperCollins*Publishers*

To Beatrice Burch

In whose desert house this book took shape

Acknowledgements

Every book originates and is produced through the efforts of people beyond the author. In my case three specific people fulfilled particular tasks that enabled this work to be completed. Victor Shupp, with whom I shared many conversations on this topic, helped me clarify my thoughts and feelings. Roy M. Carlisle, my editor at Harper & Row San Francisco, helped structure and organize this book as he did my previous two books, *We* and *Inner Work*. He also introduced me to Naomi Lucks who, through her writing skills, helped construct and polish the drafts of the manuscript. She also followed through on particular points of research pertinent to the myth of Dionysus and my accompanying commentary.

At various conferences and lectures countless friends and acquaintances, too numerous to mention, have provided insights. To all of these, including Victor, Roy, and Naomi, I offer my thanks and gratitude for their support.

FIRST HARPERCOLLINS PAPERBACK EDITION PUBLISHED IN 1989.

Library of Congress Cataloging-in-Publication Data

Johnson, Robert A., 1921–
    Ecstasy: understanding the psychology of joy.

    Bibliography: p.
    I. Joy. 2. Ecstasy. I. Title.
BF575.H27J64   1987   152.4   87-45180
ISBN 0-06-250427-4
ISBN 0-06-250432-0 (pbk.)

---

90 91 92 93 BANTA 10 9 8 7 6 5 4 3 2

Contents

The Worlds of Psychology and Myth   vi

PART I   ECSTASY: UNDERSTANDING THE
PSYCHOLOGY OF JOY   1

1. The Myth of Dionysus   5
2. What Is Ecstasy?   11
3. The Rise and Fall of Dionysus   15
4. The Other Side of Ecstasy   18
5. Celebration of Ecstasy   28
6. Women and Dionysus: Celebration of Life   33
7. Androgyny: The Union of Male and Female   37
8. The Return of the Scapegoat   43
9. Filled with Light or Filled with Air?   48
10. The God Connection   53

PART II   TOUCHING ECSTASY   61

11. Active Imagination: Meeting the Archetype   66
12. Dreamwork: Working with the Archetype   74
13. Ritual and Ceremony: Bringing Joy Home   82

Epilogue   97
Notes   99

The Worlds of Psychology and Myth

The multiplicity of the gods correspondeth to the multiplicity of man.

C. G. JUNG

Ecstasy. It was once considered a favor of the gods, a divine gift that could lift mortals out of ordinary reality and into a higher world. The transformative fire of ecstasy would burn away the barriers between ourselves and our souls, bestowing on us a greater understanding of our relation to ourselves and to the universe.

It is the great tragedy of contemporary Western society that we have virtually lost the ability to experience the transformative power of ecstasy and joy. This loss affects every aspect of our lives. We seek ecstasy everywhere, and for a moment we may think we have found it. But, on a very deep level, we remain unfulfilled.

Our materialistic society teaches us that the only reality is the one we can hold onto, the only thing of value what we can "take to the bank." Our spirits need nourishment as much as ever. But, having excluded the inner experience of divine ecstasy from our lives, we can look only for its physical equivalent. And no matter how hard we look, or how many low-grade ecstatic experiences we accumulate, we crave more.

This craving has led to the most characteristic symptom of our time: addictive behavior. So many of our lives are touched by addiction—if not our own, then that of a relative, a friend, a celebrity. Do you recognize any of these? The successful young entrepreneurs who think they need cocaine to give them the competitive edge; the supermoms who can't get through the day without a tranquilizer; the harried managers who need two or three drinks every night after work to unwind; the young children who try street drugs because they are already touched by our society's bankruptcy of feeling; the college students who go to parties solely to get drunk or stoned; the dangerously fast drivers who are addicted to the thrill of speed; the insider traders who make illegal deals on the stock market because they are addicted to the kick of making money; the perpetual singles who go from lover to lover, addicted to the first glow of romantic love.

Addiction is the negative side of spiritual seeking. We are looking for an exultation of the spirit; but instead of fulfillment we get a short-lived physical thrill that can never satisfy the chronic, gnawing emptiness with which we are beset.

To fill this emptiness, we need to reconnect with the capacity for ecstasy that lies dormant within us. Our first step must be to try to understand the nature of ecstasy.

One can often use myth to elucidate psychological processes, as I have done elsewhere. For example, my book entitled *He* explored masculine psychology through the legend of Parsifal and the Grail; *We* explored romantic love through the story of Tristan and Iseult. This book explores the nature of ecstasy through the myth of Dionysus.

In ancient Greece Dionysus was the god of wine and ecstasy. The myth of Dionysus, and the rise and fall of his cult, offer perhaps the best elucidation of our loss of the ecstatic experience.

Part I of this book explores the meaning of the Dionysian archetype of ecstasy and what its loss has meant for us. Part II suggests avenues we can explore to reclaim and express the true joy that is ours by birthright.

Archetypes: Blueprints of Human Behavior

The world of the ancient Greeks was formed and determined by their gods. In the larger-than-life actions of the gods and goddesses they saw the dramas of daily life. Today the gods of Olympus seem to have little relevance. Our world is on a more human scale, molded by psychological forces. For us, Olympus is simply a mountain.

But the fact that we no longer have the Olympic realm in which to seek the gods does not mean that the gods have ceased to exist. The forces they represent express themselves in the way that is most understandable to us: psychologically, as modes of behavior.

It is as psychologist Carl Jung once said: We do not believe in the reality of Olympus, so the ancient Greek gods live on for us today as symptoms. We no longer have the thunderbolts of Zeus, we have headaches. We no longer have the arrows of Eros, we have angina pains. We no longer have the divine ecstasy of Dionysus, we have addictive behavior. Even though we no longer recognize the gods, we experience their powerful forces.

Jung called the forces behind these symptoms *archetypes*— literally, "first patterns"—blueprints of the basic human drives and qualities that we all share. We tend to think of ourselves as unique individuals, and to a great extent we are. But we also contain within our deepest selves a plurality of these drives and behaviors, which we express in our own ways.

We see the expression of archetypes every day. For example, we may say that a particular woman is a "real earth mother" because she is nurturing, caring, and down to earth. Or we may say that an overly macho, aggressive man "thinks he's Rambo." These archetypes work well for us as descriptions of behavior. We understand immediately what they mean.

Jung considered the Greek gods to be perfect archetypes because their images were distinct and predictable. They never went against type. For example, Zeus, the chief god of Olympus, was forever falling in love. His wife, Hera, the goddess of marriage, was always jealous, always vengeful, always spiteful. It would be completely out of character for her to forgive Zeus or one of his lovers. Instead Hera always plans, plots, and executes heartless revenge. She is the archetype of the jealous wife.

The basic forms and patterns of human behavior do not change, they merely put on the clothes and mores of a particular time and place. For example, in the West we often express the psychological archetypes through our movie idols—Marilyn Monroe as the goddess of love, Venus or Aphrodite; John Wayne as the god of war, Aries or Mars. We can try to repress these archetypes, to drive them underground; but sooner or later they will reemerge. They may come back in an unfamiliar form, but they will be driven by the same archetypal energy.

Myth and the Collective Unconscious

Many modern people equate myth and untruth. As one man I know put it, "Myths and legends are the same thing, aren't they? Except that legends have a grain of truth—there really was a Johnny Appleseed—and myths are completely untrue." A great many people in our society agree with this thinking. For them, myths are stories that belong to dead cultures, "primitive" peoples, or children, and have no bearing on modern adult lives. They are sadly mistaken.

In fact, as we shall see, myths have everything to do with our lives because myths are populated by archetypes. When we read myth as Jung did, we can see clearly how our basic human drives interact. Myth then becomes a rich source of insight into our psychological motivations.

For many people myths have the quality of dreams. Both are filled with fantastic events and images, and both communicate deep psychological truths. Dreams use symbols to send messages from the unconscious self to the conscious self. In the same way a myth is a message from a deeper layer of our psyche, which we share with our whole culture. This Jung called the *collective unconscious*. When we understand a dream we contact a hidden portion of ourselves. When we contact the inner meaning of a myth we touch all humanity, because each of us shares in the rich images of the collective unconscious.

It might help you to think of the collective unconscious as a great sea from which we have all been born. In this sea live the feelings, ideas, abilities, behaviors, faults, and virtues that we identify as ourselves; and out of this sea each individual conscious self, each *ego*, each "I" is born. Even when we feel most isolated from others, it is important to remember that our common psychological home remains the same. The collective unconscious is the source of our spiritual and psychological nourishment, the material of which our inner lives are made. Of this Jung said,

> For indeed our consciousness does not create itself—it wells up from unknown depths. In childhood it awakens gradually, and all through life it wakes each morning out of the depths of sleep from an unconscious condition. It is like a child that is born daily out of the primordial womb of the unconscious.*

Through the drama of myth and its archetypal actors we can share in the wisdom of the collective unconscious, which has been preserved for us through the centuries.

Communicating with Our Unconscious

When a myth transcends mere storytelling and truly comes alive for us, we experience deep psychological understanding. By learning to identify these archetypes and understand them as processes at work within ourselves, we can make real personal change. When we begin to understand myths on this deep level we open up communication between our conscious and unconscious selves, gaining important insights and enriching our lives.

How do these two very different selves communicate? Jung once observed that the ego has the same relationship to the collective unconscious as a cork does to the ocean on which it floats, with one important exception: *The ego has consciousness.* It can make a dialogue with the unconscious. In this dialogue we can begin to make a step on the journey toward wholeness.

---

*Sources for quotations can be found at the back of the book.

The basic forms and patterns of human behavior do not change, they merely put on the clothes and mores of a particular time and place. For example, in the West we often express the psychological archetypes through our movie idols—Marilyn Monroe as the goddess of love, Venus or Aphrodite; John Wayne as the god of war, Aries or Mars. We can try to repress these archetypes, to drive them underground; but sooner or later they will reemerge. They may come back in an unfamiliar form, but they will be driven by the same archetypal energy.

Myth and the Collective Unconscious

Many modern people equate myth and untruth. As one man I know put it, "Myths and legends are the same thing, aren't they? Except that legends have a grain of truth—there really was a Johnny Appleseed—and myths are completely untrue." A great many people in our society agree with this thinking. For them, myths are stories that belong to dead cultures, "primitive" peoples, or children, and have no bearing on modern adult lives. They are sadly mistaken.

In fact, as we shall see, myths have everything to do with our lives because myths are populated by archetypes. When we read myth as Jung did, we can see clearly how our basic human drives interact. Myth then becomes a rich source of insight into our psychological motivations.

For many people myths have the quality of dreams. Both are filled with fantastic events and images, and both communicate deep psychological truths. Dreams use symbols to send messages from the unconscious self to the conscious self. In the same way a myth is a message from a deeper layer of our psyche, which we share with our whole culture. This Jung called the *collective unconscious*. When we understand a dream we contact a hidden portion of ourselves. When we contact the inner meaning of a myth we touch all humanity, because each of us shares in the rich images of the collective unconscious.

It might help you to think of the collective unconscious as a clouds. We, on the other hand, might fly a small plane into the sky, seed the clouds, and cause the rain ourselves. The tribal people will exert all the power they can muster to effect change on an unconscious level. A modern people will completely bypass the unconscious, because for them it is not "real." As a result we tend to make changes that are expedient but not necessarily prudent. Because we consider only our immediate needs, and not the needs of the whole system, we have no idea what unconscious forces we are setting into motion and what the long-term consequences of our actions will be.

To remedy this error, we must bring myth back into the realm of subjects suitable for adult consideration. We must learn to accord the inner world described in myth the same respect we give the outer world described by science. When we can understand and accept myth as a living picture of our inner world, we will be on our way to effecting real change.

PART I

ECSTASY:
UNDERSTANDING THE
PSYCHOLOGY OF JOY

Ecstasy: Understanding the Psychology of Joy

Joy, divine spark of the Gods,
daughter of Elysium,
we enter your sanctuary,
drunk with fire.
Your magic reunites
what custom has sternly parted.
All men become brothers
where your gentle wings rest.

SCHILLER'S ODE TO JOY

Ecstasy—the Dionysian experience—may be intellectually unfamiliar. But in ecstatic expression we will recognize a long-forgotten part of ourselves that makes us truly alive and connects us with every living thing. In Greek myth that part of ourselves is represented by Dionysus.

As you read the myth of Dionysus in the next chapter, remember that it is a picture of the forces, behaviors, and instincts that shape our inner world. Dionysus is a complex figure who symbolizes the irrational world of our senses as it interacts with the rational world of rules and limitations.

Half-mortal, half-god, Dionysus had more epiphanies—more manifestations—than any other god. He could change his shape from lion to stag to goat to panther to man to god. Dynamic, powerful, ever changing, all these manifestations are valid representations of the archetype. In the myth you will meet many aspects of Dionysus: Dionysus the personification of divine ecstasy, who can bring transcendent joy or madness; Dionysus the goat—the capricious, unpredictable thrill of joy that makes us jump up and click our heels; Dionysus the personification of wine and its ability to bring either spiritual transcendence or physical addiction.

If this does not seem to you like the "ordinary" Greek god, you are not far off. The dynamic, volatile Dionysus was unique among the Olympians:

The characteristic of an Olympian god (patriarchal) in contrast to a mystery god (matriarchal) is that the Olympian form is rigidly fixed, and always human. He has lost his animal forms and his magical ability to transmute from one energy shape to anther. . . . The Olympian is idealized, rational, aloof, deathless—and so ultimately he seems too *geometric* to move us. . . . The Olympian does not evolve, he apotheosizes—to the blare of trumpets. This means he is not born from woman, or earth, or matter, but from his own absolute will. He represents a static perfection, in human form, incapable of transformation or ecstatic change; as a god, he is an intellectual concept. And so the energy exchange between all creatures and their magical-evolutionary power connection is broken: God becomes mere idea, and his world mere mechanism.

With all this in mind, let us read the myth of Dionysus. When you hear the story of his birth, you will wonder how he ever survived at all.

1. The Myth of Dionysus

I am Dionysus, the son of Zeus,
come back to Thebes, this land where I was born.
My mother was Cadmus' daughter, Semele by name,
midwived by fire, delivered by lightning's
blast.
  And here I stand, a god incognito,
disguised as a man . . .

EURIPIDES, THE BACCHAE

No other Greek god came into the world in quite the same way as Dionysus. His father was Zeus, whose name means "shower of light." Lord of the sky, god of the thunderbolt, Zeus was the most powerful of all the gods of Olympus. He loved women, mortal and immortal, and enjoyed many love affairs. His wife, the goddess Hera, was naturally angry and jealous. She was forever seeking revenge for Zeus's many love affairs—and a goddess scorned has fury indeed!

Born of Fire*

One day Zeus was traveling on earth. He wore a disguise, because undisguised no mortal could look at him and live. He came to Thebes, an ancient city of Greece, where he fell hopelessly in love with Semele, the daughter of King Cadmus. Their passion was great, and before long she became pregnant.

Semele wanted nothing more than to look into the true eyes of her lover. She was urged on mercilessly by her nurse—who happened to be the treacherous Hera in disguise. Finally, Semele could stand it no longer. She asked Zeus to grant her a boon.

---

*The story of Dionysus has been told for thousands of years. There will naturally be changes from retelling to retelling.

Zeus was in a good mood, and he loved the young woman. Foolishly, he swore an unbreakable oath on the River Styx that she could have whatever she asked.

When the innocent Semele asked to see the god of the thunderbolt in his true splendor, Zeus was horrified. He knew that the sight of his godhead would mean her certain death.

"No!" he cried in anguish. "Anything but that. You do not know what you are asking for." But she persisted and Zeus sadly kept his word. As he shed his disguise and revealed his fiery radiance, the unfortunate Semele was almost completely incinerated. Only her womb, around which she had wrapped some ivy, escaped the flame. (Ivy is said to be the only thing on earth that is impervious to the splendor of god.)

Zeus was furious. Quickly, he plucked the fetus from the womb, cut an incision in his own thigh, and tucked the child into it.

The baby continued to grow in Zeus's thigh. When gestation was complete Zeus gave birth to the infant god Dionysus.

This child of fire was a brand new force to be reckoned with. Even the Titans—the powerful first gods of earth, who represented the instinctive masculine qualities—were quaking in their boots. Brutally, they tore the baby to pieces and boiled him for good measure. They weren't going to have anything like this coming into the world!

But Dionysus would not stay dead. A pomegranate tree, symbol of fertility, sprouted from the earth where a drop of his blood had fallen; and Zeus's mother, Rhea, made Dionysus whole once again. In this way the young god was born three times: once from his mortal mother's womb; once from his immortal father's thigh; and once from the wisdom of the earth, represented by his grandmother. With a start like this, one wonders what kind of a god we have on hand!

The Young God

Semele's sister Ino and her husband, Athamas, raised the baby Dionysus as a girl so that Hera would not recognize him.

But the goddess was not deceived, and in her rage she drove the aunt and uncle mad.

Zeus acted quickly. He ordered Hermes, the divine messenger, to transform Dionysus temporarily into a young goat and bring him to the beautiful Mount Nysa. There he would be raised secretly by nymphs, the joyous female spirits of the forests and mountains.

The nymphs loved their young charge. They housed him in a cave and fed him on honey. Dionysus spent his childhood gamboling freely over the mountainside, surrounded by the glories of nature and learning the sensuous pleasures of the earth. His teachers were many and varied: The Muses inspired him with poetry and music. The satyrs, half-man, half-goat, taught him the wonders of dance and exuberant sexuality. The sileni, part-horse, part-man, spirits of the springs and rivers, taught him wisdom. Silenus, the intoxicated old man who was Dionysus's predecessor, taught the young god virtue.

Dionysus passed the years happily, learning many things. Like the grapevine, which can only grow in the sun's intense heat and the moisture of the spring rain, Dionysus had been born of fire and nourished by the rains of the mountain. He understood the power of the vine perfectly, and marked his passage from childhood to young godhood by inventing the art of winemaking (some say he learned it from Silenus), which would bring humanity so much potential joy and desperation.

At last Dionysus stood revealed as a god. This was just what the ever-vengeful Hera had been waiting for. Recognizing Dionysus at last, she cursed him with madness.

The Travels of Dionysus

The raving Dionysus left his home on Mount Nysa and began to travel the world. Mad as he was, Dionysus was still a powerful god. Wherever he went he spread the art of winemaking and his own worship.

He was accompanied by a startling array of followers: His tutor, the fat old drunkard Silenus, rode precariously on a donkey; grinning satyrs, joyous nymphs, prancing centaurs, and other woodland spirits capered and danced alongside. For human followers he had the Maenads. These wild women of the mountains, initiates of the ancient women's mysteries, worshiped their god with singing, dancing, and bloody feasts. Together, they cut a swath of wild and joyous celebration across the ancient world.

In time Rhea purified the young god of his madness and initiated him into her mysteries, the very secret women's mysteries. The power of Dionysus was then unparalleled.

Wherever Dionysus went he invited people to join in his celebration. One thing soon became clear: Those who chose to worship him experienced divine ecstasy; those who opposed him chose madness.

Kings were especially prone to oppose Dionysus, who seemed the antithesis of law and order. When Dionysus invaded Thrace (an area which is now divided between Greece and Turkey) King Lycurgus fought violently against him and captured the god's army. Dionysus went into hiding deep under the sea with Thetis, an ocean nymph.

Rhea struck Lycurgus with madness and the raving king hacked his son Dryas to death, believing him to be a grapevine. The very soil of Thrace recoiled from the horror and became barren.

At this moment Dionysus emerged triumphantly from the sea and announced that Thrace would not flourish unless Lycurgus was killed. The people of Thrace rushed to obey. They tied horses to the king's arms and legs and pulled him limb from limb.

King Pentheus of Thebes—Dionysus's own cousin—fared no better. Dionysus asked the Theben women to join in his worship, proclaiming himself a new god. King Pentheus was offended by this wild band and ordered Dionysus and his followers arrested.

Teiresius, the old, blind prophet who knew the will of the gods, warned Pentheus that Dionysus was exactly what he claimed to be: a new and important god. But Pentheus mocked Teiresius and denied Dionysus to his face.

The King's men found it impossible to imprison the god and his followers, and Dionysus and his wild band of celebrants escaped to the hills.

Pentheus pursued them in a blind fury, accompanied by many of the women of Thebes—his own mother and aunts among them. The women went mad and, thinking Pentheus was a wild beast, they tore him to pieces in a frenzy of bloodlust.

It was certainly unwise to refuse to worship Dionysus. When three young women of Orchomenus declined his offer, he drove them mad by changing shape from a girl, to a lion, to a bull, to a panther. Eventually the women were themselves turned into birds.

In another shape-changing story, Dionysus demonstrates another facet of his power. One day some pirates sailing near Greece spotted a young man sitting near the shore. He was so handsome that they thought he must surely be a nobleman and worth a hefty ransom. Filled with greed, they captured him and brought him on board.

They tried to tie him up to prevent his escape but found, as had Pentheus, that the ropes would not hold their knots. Only one crew member, the helmsman, realized that they must have captured a god. He begged the others to let him go. But the rest of the crew refused.

Then something extraordinary happened. Wind blew and filled the sails, but the ship did not move. In a terrifying yet glorious moment, rivers of wine began to stream over the deck; grapevines grew in wild profusion over the sail; and ivy, fruit, and flowers twined up the mast. Dionysus transformed himself into a lion. The terrified crew members jumped overboard and were changed into dolphins in midair. Only the helmsman, who had recognized the god, was spared.

Dionysus continued sailing the waters near Greece. One day, on the island of Naxos, he found Ariadne, the daughter of

King Minos of Crete. The beautiful young woman had been abandoned there by her husband, Theseus. Ariadne and Dionysus fell in love and soon married, and their wedding was attended by the gods. Their marriage was a perfect union. They never quarreled, and they had many children. In the end, however, the mortal Ariadne died. In her memory Dionysus placed her crown among the stars, where it can be seen today as the Corona Borealis.

Dionysus on Olympus

The tales of Dionysian ecstasy and madness spread across the world, and soon the power of Dionysus was recognized from Asia to Africa to Europe. Eventually, Hestia, the ancient and respected goddess of the hearth, stepped down and gave him her seat on Olympus. He sat thereafter at the right hand of his father, Zeus.

Dionysus, beloved and on Olympus at last, was happy but for one thing: He wanted to see his mother, whom he had never known. He decided to make one more voyage.

Braving death, he rescued Semele from the underworld and brought her to Olympus to live with the immortals. He renamed her Thyone, which means "ecstasy."

Here the myth officially ends. But Dionysus did not live happily ever after. He was eventually ejected from Olympus by mortal politicians, suppressed by Romans, Jews, and Christians alike.

Forced into the realm of dream and myth, his energy is once again returning to our consciousness. If we go willingly to meet and understand Dionysus, we can use this archetypal power to transform our lives.

2. What Is Ecstasy?

"Ecstasy's not the right word at all," says the brother-in-law, who has been thinking about it. "It makes you think of some . . . mun*dane* ecstasy."

JOAN DIDION

Dionysus has been called the most important of the Greek gods. Certainly he is the most misunderstood! The very profusion of his names and qualities makes immediate comprehension difficult. He is called the god of wine, the god of abandon, the great liberator, the god of ecstasy. He represents the continual rebirth of life in the spring, the irrational wisdom of the senses, and the soul's transcendence.

He is not a straightforward, thundering sky god like Zeus, or a messenger between the worlds like Hermes. Unlike the static, abstract Olympians, Dionysus embodies the continual, unpredictable changes and transmutations of nature. Like the vine he is born of fire, torn apart, seemingly dead, and always reborn. At once a tragic and heroic figure, like the wine he represents he brings humans both madness and ecstasy.

Western civilization praises the orderly life. We have a healthy skepticism that insists "seeing is believing." Our world is built on thinking, logic, progress, and success, and within these limits we feel secure. But today even our scientists tell us that these limits are illusory. Quantum physics shows us "the *dancing universe;* the ceaseless flow of energy going through an infinite variety of patterns." This is the Dionysian energy, the dance of the Maenads, the power of life that flows through all of us and unites us with heaven and earth.

You may not have identified it as such, but you have probably consciously touched Dionysian energy in your life: When you look into a loved one's eyes and feel for a moment love that is beyond time and space; when you spontaneously shout for joy and feel the positive, invigorating energy charging every cell of your body. Unfortunately, we spend so much time trying to understand the world and ourselves intellectually that we have virtually cut ourselves off from the spontaneous, guilt-free experience of our emotional and irrational natures. We have almost forgotten that such a thing can exist.

Dionysian ecstasy is found in the *sensuous* world, the world of poets and artists and dreamers, who show us the life of the spirit as seen through the senses. Do not confuse this with the sensual world, the materialistic world of pleasure that is destitute of spirit. The sensual world is the one we see all around us: the pursuit of money for its own sake, the desperate chasing after empty pleasures. The sensuous world is filled with the profusion of nature's fruits; it is the divine realm, the garden of the gods. What a beautiful thing! If one can make the translation from the sensual world, devoid of spirit, to the sensuous world of Dionysus, then one can begin a new era in one's life.

Dionysian Language

Part of our difficulty in understanding the Dionysian experience has to do with the words we associate with it. Let's try to understand them in a new way.

Irrational

Dionysus and his world we describe as *irrational*, which we usually take to be a negative term. We generally think of an irrational person as strange, offbeat, or insane; and of an irrational statement as incorrect. But the original meaning of irrational knowledge is simply knowledge gained through our senses rather than through our rational thought processes. The Dionysian way is to see the world instinctively, on a sensuous, intuitive level rather than in an abstract, logical, once-removed way.

Dionysian

The very adjective *Dionysian* has uncomfortable associations for most people. When you hear something described as Dionysian, do you think to yourself, "Ah, the ecstatic principle! The transcendent nature of the soul!" Probably not. You are more likely to respond indignantly, "Dionysian? What are you suggesting? A wild, drunken orgy? People tearing their clothes off, getting drunk, sleeping with everyone else? Do you want me to lose my job and my marriage in one night?"

Orgy

Poor Dionysus! He really has been given a bad name. Few people know that the word *orgy*, which evokes such an emotional response, originally meant "ritual worship of the god Dionysus." It was a sacred, not profane, expression of the love of god.

Ecstasy and Joy

In the West the word *ecstasy* is likely to evoke thoughts of X-rated movies. But this very misunderstood term comes from the root *ex stasis*—to stand outside oneself. If I say, "I am ecstatic! I am simply beside myself!" I mean that I am filled with an emotion too powerful for my body to contain or my rational mind to understand. I am transported to another realm in which I am able to experience ecstasy. When the followers of Dionysus drank the god's wine they stepped for a moment outside their daily lives and experienced spiritual ecstasy.

I am sorry to say that we rarely stand outside ourselves these days. The world is too much with us. We are constantly working, thinking, planning, doing—what to eat, where to go, how to support our families, who to vote for. All the responsibility and power we burden ourselves with! We can't bear it for very long without breaking down in some way. We need some relief from all that strength; to be for a moment in that timeless, spaceless, primal place which has no responsibility, which isn't going anywhere. We need to stand outside ourselves and experience the flow of life, the Dionysian energy.

Joy is another Dionysian attribute that we have managed to water down. We hear the word in Christmas carols—"Joy to the World!" We read it in books—*The Joy of Cooking*, *The Joy of Sex*. But what does it really mean?

A friend once paid me a high compliment. "Robert," he said, "you're one of the few people I know who ever uses the word 'joy.'" Nonplussed, I replied, "Oh?" and that was the end of the conversation. But he'd pricked my curiosity. When I thought about it, I realized that I had no idea what the word meant. So off I went to the dictionary, where I found one of those fine differentiations in pairs of words that are so valuable to me.

To my surprise I found that "happiness" was defined as "a happening of chance, luck, fortune." The word "joy," on the other hand, was defined as "an exultation of the spirit, gladness, delight, the beatitude of heaven or paradise." That's quite a difference! Happiness is always short-lived. We are constantly chasing after this experience; we think that we should be happy—after all, isn't the pursuit of happiness guaranteed to us in the Bill of Rights? But happiness comes at the whim of fortune. No happiness can be kept permanently.

So ask yourself this question: Do you want happiness, which is luck or fortune? Or do you want joy, which is the beatitude of paradise? These two are so close, and the differentiation is so crucial: because to seek joy is to seek Dionysus.

3. The Rise and Fall of Dionysus

Man is concerned with man, and forgets the whole and the flowing.
EZRA POUND

How did we lose Dionysus? Psychologically, the story of his loss is the triumph of rationality over irrationality; thinking over feeling; the concrete "masculine" ideals of power, aggression, and progress over the intangible "feminine" values of receptivity, growth, and nurturing. As the patriarchal religions gained in power, the old matrifocal ways of Dionysus were diminished and finally lost.

As early as the thirteenth century B.C. the worship of Dionysus had spread across Europe and Asia. His cult received the official stamp of approval in the late sixth and early fifth centuries B.C., when he replaced Hestia on Olympus.

The ancient Greeks celebrated Dionysus's festival in springtime, when the grapevine was just beginning to leaf. It was a celebration like no other. For five days all business came to a halt. No one could be arrested, and some prisoners were even freed. Perhaps most unusual, his worship was not confined to a temple ritual. Instead, they honored him with a sacred play. It is to this celebration of Dionysus's death and rebirth that we owe the classical Greek theater. The joyous celebration of his resurrection gave birth to comedy; and the bemoaning of his death—the singing over the sacrifice of the symbolic goat, the tragōidia, or "goat song"—became tragedy.

His glory, however, was not to last. The patriarchal, law-abiding religions of the Romans, Jews, and Christians who succeeded the Greeks did not take kindly to the irrational antics and intoxications of Dionysus.

When the Romans got hold of the capricious, goatlike quality of Dionysus they perverted it quickly and totally. They made Dionysus into Bacchus—no longer the god of wine, but the god of drunkenness. Around A.D. 186 the Romans began systematically to persecute Dionysus and his followers, the Bacchantes, who were perceived as threats to the Roman system. The Bacchantes were charged with immoralities and crimes, and—in a madness similar to that which swept the Salem witch trials in colonial America—the government executed thousands of innocent people. The Roman senate finally banned the Bacchanalia—which had formerly been the Dionysian festivals—and Dionysus has not been seen in polite company since.

In his place the Romans elevated Apollo, the god of light, who had at one time been honored equally with Dionysus at Delphi. Apollo gradually came to represent analytical thought and the preservation of law and order. The unpredictable, irrational, ecstatic Dionysus had no place in this scheme— was, in fact, the enemy of it. The chief god was now officially to be found "up there" in the sky as the sun, Apollo. "Down here," the earth, the realm of Dionysus, was shorn of its power. As we shall see later, Dionysus fared no better with the Jews or the Christians, who turned his goat image into the very face of the devil.

This is the historical version of the rise and fall of Dionysus. But there are other reasons for his loss. Sometimes, psychologically, it is necessary to set one quality aside so that another may be adequately rooted. This is the case with Dionysus. The collective human psyche needed to suppress the irrational before it got completely out of hand, in order to nurture the rational. As greatly as I feel his loss, I also believe that had the Dionysian ethic prevailed we could never have achieved the discipline we needed to make the progress which our scientific, rational culture has produced.

Now, however, the cult of rationality seems to have gone as

far as it can go. The loss of spiritual ecstasy in Western society has left a void that we fill in the only way we know how: with danger and excitement.

4. The Other Side of Ecstasy

Sporadic violence in several Bay Area communities blemished the promise of the New Year yesterday as residents began 1987 by shooting, stabbing, and bombing one another.

SAN FRANCISCO CHRONICLE, JANUARY 2, 1987

Dionysus lives in some strange places these days. He lives in the thrill we experience when we read about the latest terrorist bombing, the latest arson fire, the latest political assassination. As we sit calmly reading our morning paper we hear a screech of brakes and a crash. Unbidden, we feel an enormous rush of energy. Cold chills go up and down our spine, we say, "How awful!"—and run outside to see the accident. This is poor-quality Dionysus; this is what happens to a basic human drive that has not been lived out for nearly four thousand years.

When Lycurgus drove the armies of Dionysus from his country he thought that he had gotten rid of this troublesome god for good. But Dionysus had merely gone into hiding deep beneath the sea. And when he reemerged it was with a violence terrifyingly powerful because it was the other side of another powerful quality: ecstasy.

Like the unfortunate Lycurgus we can refuse to recognize an archetype for as long as we wish; but, like Dionysus in hiding under the sea, it will not disappear. If we do not invest it with our humanity it will return to us in a dehumanized form, still charged with the same archetypal energy, but manifesting itself in a much more primitive way. In this chilling commentary Jungian psychologist Marie Louise von Franz explains how our refusal to honor an ethical, caring human drive can transform it into something wild and destructive:

. . . what would it mean if an impulse appeared in a dream as a wolf, or a tiger [or perhaps as a goat]? Here a psychological content has been wrongfully pushed into the body side and has been perverted so that it is no longer strictly human. It is a fact that if an impulse comes up and is not lived out, then it goes back down and tends to develop anti-human qualities. What should have been a human impulse becomes a tiger-like impulse.

For instance, a man has a feeling impulse to say something positive to someone, and he blocks it off through inhibition. He might tend to dream that he has driven over a child with his car. He had a spontaneous feeling impulse on the level of his child, and his conscious purpose smashed it. The human is still there, but as a hurt child. Should he do that habitually for five years, he would no longer dream of a child who had been hurt, but of a zoo full of raging wild animals in a cage. An impulse which is driven back loads up with energy and becomes inhuman.

You cannot kill a god, who is by definition immortal. Neither can you kill an archetype, for an archetype is a basic human drive. We carry the archetypes deep within us; they are integral parts of our human nature that must be lived out. When an archetype is not lived out with consciousness or dignity, as von Franz says, it "loads up with energy and becomes inhuman."

This happens not only on the level of the individual, but on the level of the collective unconscious, the psyche of a whole society. Carl Jung has said of this phenomenon:

The gigantic catastrophes that threaten us are not elemental happenings of a physical or biological kind, but are psychic events. We are threatened in a fearful way by wars and revolutions that are nothing else than psychic epidemics. At any moment a few million people may be seized by a madness, and then we have another world war or a devastating revolution. Instead of being exposed to wild beasts, tumbling rocks, and inundating waters, man is exposed today to the elemental forces of his own psyche.

This was brought home to me one day when a friend took me to an air show. Thousands of people were in the crowd— I'd never been to such a thing before. My friend said, "You know, there's a tremendous amount of collective power in a group like this. They will demand blood, and they're strong enough to get it." At that very moment a small plane crashed and burned right in front of us. I could feel the Dionysian energy galvanize the crowd, which was at once thrilled and horrified. It was a terrible form, but nonetheless the god was served.

Looking for Ecstasy in All the Wrong Places

Our society esteems thinking and doing, progress and success, above all else. We go straight ahead, aiming for the top, looking out for number one in all our endeavors. If a given thing does not have a monetary value, or show a concrete return, we will probably place it lower on the scale. We tend to like those things we can control, and dislike what we can't control or understand.

These are the values of our patriarchal society, with its emphasis on power and acquisition, and it has won many fine prizes for us. Without our love for discovery, facts, science, progress, and innovation we would certainly not have all the medical advances that save lives, or the machinery that makes our daily routine so much easier. All this, however, has been won at the expense of less tangible qualities—feeling and intuition, caring and nurturing, empathy and receptivity—the Dionysian qualities. We tend to devalue them because they do not show concrete rewards.

Craving spiritual ecstasy, we mistakenly seek material fulfillment. We chase after a phantom, and when we catch it—in the form of more money, more food, more sex, more drugs, more drinks, more oblivion—we find that we have been chasing ephemeral happiness when we should have invited lasting joy.

What do we do next? We use all the intellectual power at our command to fill the void. We read books and take classes, looking for "the answer." But the answer can be found only in the sensuous world of Dionysus, and we have forgotten where that is.

Dionysian Malnutrition

We have chosen the quick fix over the spiritual nutrition of Dionysian energy, and we are starving because of it. I was vividly reminded of this by the following story.

A British doctor ran across an interesting paradox. Indian Hindus in their usual diet don't get enough vitamin B_{12} to keep a rabbit alive, yet in general they do not suffer from B_{12} deficiency. How could this be? The doctor decided that either his understanding of how much B_{12} the body needed was in error, or that the Hindus' diet included more B_{12} than tests indicated it did. So he went to India to study the problem more closely, and found that the data were completely at odds. No, there was not enough B_{12} in the Hindu diet to keep a rabbit alive; yet the Hindus were doing well. Was it climate? Psychology? The doctor brought a Hindu man back to London with him so that he could perform more clinically precise tests in his own laboratory.

He fed the Hindu exactly the same diet in England as the man had eaten in India, and quite soon the man came down with vitamin B_{12} deficiency. What had happened? It turned out that the English food was *too clean*. There were enough weevils in the flour and worms in the fruit of India to give the Hindus the bare minimum of B_{12} they needed to survive. But in the sanitized food of England there was not enough to meet even minimum daily requirements.

This is exactly what we have done with Dionysus. We have cleansed him out of our consciousness, denied him on moral grounds; and we are the worse for it. Like the weevils in the flour and the worms in the fruit, we get just enough poor-quality Dionysus—through auto accidents and screaming headlines, terrorism and street violence, drinking and drugs—

to give us the little bit of ecstatic quality we need to keep alive.

But, as with any addiction, we need more and more and more. Because we are not getting the divine joy we actually need to satisfy us, we crave its opposite. Thus robberies become muggings, muggings become beatings, beatings become shootings, shootings become bombings, and where will it end? This is the addictive behavior that plagues our society and touches every aspect of our lives.

Sensation and Materialism

When Western society chose to follow the erratic footsteps of the degraded Bacchus instead of the joyful dance of Dionysus, it began to confuse materialism with sensation. As a result we citizens of the late twentieth century can truly be said to have lost our senses—or at least to have lost contact with them.

Even the clothes we wear tell us something is amiss. Both men and women today "dress for success" by wearing ties—in effect separating their heads, their thinking processes, from the rest of their bodies and thus symbolically cutting off sensation below their necks. When they take their ties off at the end of the day they go wild. All that bottled-up sensation comes rushing out looking for somewhere to go.

At first glance, I suppose, our society looks terribly sensation oriented—the flashing neon signs of Broadway, the almost naked bodies on billboards, our obsession with food and exercise. Originally, perhaps, we want these things for the pleasurable sensations they give us. But after a while we develop a craving for sheer quantity and lose sight of quality all together. So it seems that we are *materially* oriented, and that is a fine distinction to make. We want more things—more cars, more money, more clothes, more drugs, more fun—but we're frightened of touch, of making real contact with another person. We're more likely to take our clothes off in front of a stranger than we are to let down our emotional defenses in front of someone we love. This unease with human contact is a reflection of the absence of good-quality Dionysus, and it has been a great loss for our society.

Never did I experience this loss more vividly than during a visit I made to Grace Episcopal Cathedral in San Francisco soon after the custom of the passing of the peace had been instigated in the Episcopal church. Robed and gloved ushers came down from the altar and shook hands with the person at the beginning of each row of pews, and this "peace" was then to be handed down from person to person until the end of the row was reached.

Well, the woman to my right was clearly horrified by this plan. She couldn't bear to touch a stranger. The Dionysian quality of being close was forbidden to her. She turned around to me with an anguished look on her face, proffered a gloved hand, and stiffly put out her little finger. I took the little finger and shook it carefully with my thumb and forefinger. The pained embarrassment at having to touch was vividly expressed between us.

I don't get angry very often, but for some reason the anger just welled up in me over this. So I turned around to the man on my left, raised him up with a big bear hug, and sat him down again. The poor man was so embarrassed that he sat there staring straight in front of him, and the peace went no farther.

This is our general, official, and especially religious attitude toward sensation: Nice people don't do it. As for feelings, yes, you may have feelings, as long as they are very discreet and totally under control. (I can't help contrasting this attitude with that of the Muslim world. There, if you are talking with a man and you stray farther than six inches from his face while you are conversing, this is a public announcement of an insult. It means you don't like him. Of course if you get within six inches of most Westerners, they become exceedingly uneasy and slowly begin to back up in an effort to increase the distance!)

Today, just as that woman and I could find no dignified way to exchange a human touch, as a society we have no respectful, dignified way to touch Dionysus. In the same way that my passing of the peace was transformed almost instantaneously into the passing of anger, our hunger for the sensuous Dionysian experience is transformed almost instantaneously into a search for sensuality. Thus we cannot find the humanized archetype because we are looking in the wrong place and in the wrong way.

Intimacy

We often bemoan the "loss of intimacy" in our society. We are quick to take a stranger to bed, but we are loathe to be touched emotionally. When we lost the concept of touch as a way to contact the god, we became ashamed of our natural urges and guilty even for our fantasies.

Perhaps we most deeply fear the loss of ecstasy because implicit in it is a loss of control. Surrender, even to the divine, is something our culture does not encourage. Surrender to the divine means crossing over from our well-defined roles and worlds into the realm of the gods, where everything is possible and nothing is explained. We have no idea what to expect, and so we are afraid. As the poet T. S. Eliot said in *Murder in the Cathedral*, we "fear the hand at the window, the fire in the thatch . . . less than we fear the love of God." Truly to experience ecstasy, the love of God, would mean to invite profound change, and this we are unwilling to do.

We run after sex, chasing the god again, but so often we get the dehumanized, poor-quality Dionysian experience. Poor-quality Dionysus expressed sexually is a terrible thing to behold. Instead of lovemaking we get rape, or sexual acts completely devoid of spirit. Just as we try to cut off our heads from the rest of our bodies, we have tried to separate our sexuality from the rest of our lives. We have even given sex its own section of town. Here, in the hours of darkness, what passes for sexual abandon in the twentieth century flashes its lights and plays its music. Our metaphors for sex are filled with energy, but the energy does not strive upward. We say, get it on, get it off, do it to me. This low-grade ecstasy is enough to keep us going, but it does not lead to transcendence.

To drown our guilt and shut down the voices we anesthetize ourselves with alcohol and drugs—ironically, in other times and places these substances were divine sacraments used to bring visions of God. With no sacred means of expression, we can express our need for Dionysus only symptomatically: through substance abuse, child molesting and domestic violence, muggings, wars, terrorism, madness.

Intoxication

Dionysus is the god of wine and ecstasy, liberation and abandon. He is the perennial profusion of color and life and energy. When we touch Dionysus we touch the irrational wisdom of the senses and experience joy.

Because we have disallowed ourselves this experience, however, we get the darker side of intoxication, a confusion of the senses that is far from spiritual. With the first sip of wine we leave the everyday world and enter a new world. We are flushed with warmth and happiness, free to enjoy ourselves. We are still in control, but feel able to let go of our burdens. This is the point at which the followers of Dionysus stopped—in fact, some of them never drank wine at all. They needed to be conscious to experience divine ecstasy—you can't be joyous and dead drunk at the same time! Unfortunately, when we replaced Dionysus with the drunkard Bacchus, we forgot when to stop.

Dionysus himself got drunk only once, and he didn't like it. To cure his wine-induced madness he went for a visit to Zeus's shrine. One story has it that he bogged down in quicksand and was saved by a donkey, who took him raving and drunk— but safe nonetheless—to Zeus. As recompense Zeus gave the donkey human speech. The other story, which I like much better, is that Dionysus turned into a donkey and arrived at Zeus's shrine braying, which became human speech. So when we get drunk enough to get this jackass aspect going, we are no longer candidates for ecstasy. Our humanness is lost.

Instead of taking the opportunity to transcend the material world, we keep drinking (or taking drugs, or trying to make money, or falling in love) to regain that first flush of happiness, which we mistook for joy. Chase it as we might, however, happiness is by nature an ephemeral experience. As we drink we become louder, looser, less in control of what we say and do. In trying to hold onto happiness we slide headlong into despair. And if we continue to drink until we can drink no more, we are likely to become violent and ultimately unconscious.

Ecstasy: A New Stage

Why do we find this transcendent ecstasy such a difficult state to achieve? Perhaps because the concept is relatively new. The advent of Dionysus, the psychological archetype of ecstasy, represented a new stage in human development. The mighty Titans, first gods of the earth, had never seen his like and tried to destroy him before he even got started. He was the last god to be added to the pantheon of Olympus and the first to be torn down, which gives an idea of how new an acquisition he is for the human race. Let me illustrate this fragility with a parallel from another realm.

I am told that the color blue was the last to be added to our color sense, and it is the one most often missing in color-blind people. The color blue is never mentioned in the Old Testament; and in all of the ancient Greek writings the color blue is never used. Even the Aegean, the most vividly blue of all the seas of the world, is described by Homer as "the wine dark sea." A faculty that is so new and so easily lost means that the human race is only just evolving that capacity into something like stability. It is the same with the Dionysian experience of spiritual ecstasy. It was the last faculty to be added to our repertoire, and the one most often missing and least in our control.

Some people burst spontaneously into a less violent, more genuinely ecstatic Dionysian quality. Such outbursts, however, are characteristically short-lived. Remember the hippie movement, which degenerated from the innocence of Woodstock to the violence of Altamont in the space of a year? We may envy people who quit their jobs, give away all their money, and try to commune with nature, but ultimately we will call them crazy and get on with our lives.

It is not enough to throw the whole society over and go dance naked on the beach. Such experiments, however well intentioned, are doomed to failure. We cannot simply move from the realm of rationality to the irrational realm of Dionysus and think that everything will be solved. This is either/or thinking. Jung has said that for us the choice is no longer either/or, but either-*and*-or. We must touch Dionysus, we must bring him back into our lives in a humanized form, or in denying him we will destroy ourselves.

This is the burden that is on us now. To keep the fine points of our patriarchal world—its order, form, care, and structure—and bring the Dionysian back in to enliven it without doing a flip-flop and going to pieces. Only in this way can we begin to move toward wholeness and joy.

5. Celebration of Ecstasy

From joy springs all creation.
By it is sustained,
Towards joy it proceeds,
And to joy it returns.

MUNDAKA UPANISHAD

The Dionysian experience is immediate and galvanizing: ecstasy or madness. This may be extreme, but it corresponds closely to our real psychological and spiritual needs. Today our scrupulously clean, law-abiding religions have little place for either the love of God or the fear of God. Like the Hindu who nearly starved on the sanitized British food, we suffer the effects of spiritual malnutrition.

When we deny ourselves contact with the awe-fulness and terror of the soul, we do ourselves great damage. When we conceive of heaven as a clean, well-lighted place with pleasant harp music and bland angels, we eviscerate our religion. When there is no longer any official room in our religious observance for the ecstasy of divinity or the dark night of the soul, we experience that light and darkness in whatever way we can. In other centuries that way might have been called possession; we have chosen to express it through physical and psychological symptoms.

I once upset an audience of seminarians in this regard by insisting that neurosis is actually a low-grade religious experience. One young man jumped up and said, "Do you mean to tell me that God is to be found in those kinky things that I do at midnight, that I would die if anyone found out about, and which I haven't even gotten up the nerve to confess?" For many people our religious structure has become just that: structure devoid of meaning.

But if you look closely and with open eyes you will see that Dionysus inhabits even our most staid religious structures—an idea that may be shocking to those churchgoers who conceive of the goat Dionysus as more akin to the devil. Take a look at the Christian Communion service, for example, and you will see that a Dionysian ritual is being carried out behind the safety of the altar rail. There we have betrayal, murder, crucifixion; the god become wine. If we can understand a Communion service as it really is—the inner meaning, not the outer structure—we will be so frightened and chills will go down our spines so violently that we will have to be transformed—which, after all, is the point of the ritual.

I recently witnessed a particularly compelling form of such a transformation in India. Like all traditional non-European societies, India has kept an honored place for Dionysian expression. (The god Siva is the chief carrier of Dionysus, but Dionysus also lives in the sensuous life of Krishna.) One day I made a visit to the temple of Tiruvanamalai and found myself confronted with a dancing Dionysus who took my breath away.

I saw a young man, accompanied by two drummers, cracking a long leather whip with explosive force. He made a great deal of sound with his whip, the drums beat louder and faster, and he danced a wild, sensuous step. A moment later he made another crack of the whip, which was aimed to dig out a chunk of flesh from his arm or chest. Blood flowed, agony was on his face. Then he danced his pain into an ecstatic state with a fury and energy I had never witnessed before. His face was transformed from pain to ecstasy by his dance.

After several of these flagellations (there are Christian parallels to this in the flagellants of the medieval church) he went to the shopkeepers around the temple asking for coins. The tradition is that one man takes on the task of inviting pain to himself and dancing it into ecstasy so that the community can be freed of this suffering. The community then provides the living for the dancer.

His dance was too raw and rough for my Western eyes, but I was aware that I had witnessed the Dionysian principle of the transformation of suffering into ecstasy in so direct a form as to take my breath away.

Dionysus and Western Christianity

To follow Dionysus is to enter the realm of the spirit, to experience the ecstasy of union with the divine. In John 6:53–54 Jesus says, "Truly, truly I say to you, unless you eat the flesh of the Son of man and drink his blood, you have no life in you; he who eats my flesh [bread] and drinks my blood [wine] has eternal life, and I will raise him up at the last day." In John 15:1 ff., Jesus says, "I am the vine." For the person taking Communion the bread *is* the flesh, the wine *is* the blood. The followers of Dionysus also consumed their god symbolically, as goat flesh, and drank him in the same way: as wine.

I am often asked if I see any connection between Dionysus and the expressions of Jesus, and the answer is, yes.

This is not as surprising as it may sound. Every disciplined or elaborate culture—as ours certainly is—needs a reprieve from its responsibilities. The Greeks had Dionysus to help them stand outside themselves and be free of their burdens for a moment. The Romans, who followed them, took the Dionysian principle off into an orgiastic expression, a drunken brawl, and renamed him Bacchus. Christianity came along and restored the ecstatic principle in the figure of Christ—twice-born, much as Dionysus is thrice-born. Christ is the god of love, the god of ecstasy, the visionary god. For me the figure of Jesus is a new trial at making respectable, making human, making workable the transcendent principle: that which shows us something greater than ourselves.

Anybody who has ever loved another human being knows what the incarnation is, because in human flesh we have godhood or goddesshood walking before us. A lover may "idolize" or "adore" the loved one: a man may "put a woman up on a pedestal." To experience the love of God through our senses—by loving another human being—is just as good as through any other faculty, although Christianity has certainly downplayed it. Jung once observed that we distort our principal mandala, the cross, by making the bottom longer than the arms or top. The Greeks had better sense: They made all points of the cross equal because they valued the sensuous and intellectual worlds equally. Because we diminish the senses, the lower half, we overcompensate the earthy dimension of the cross. Western Christianity is out of balance in this matter of sensation. Jesus was equally spirit and matter, but we tend not to believe that way. This quality in Jesus has been misunderstood so totally that he has, paradoxically, become the chief enemy of the Dionysian element in the Christian world.

One of the Hindu saints said, "The best way possible to worship God is simply to be happy." And we've lost that. We have looked only at Jesus' suffering and taken it to ourselves. We feel that if we do not suffer as he did, we are not good people, and we certainly will not go to heaven. I don't think it was the nature of Christ to be so repressive as Christianity has become.

Jesus and Dionysus

The Antioch chalice, a famous Christian chalice, shows Christ engaged in one of Dionysus's favorite activities—swinging on a seat of grapevines, poised between two worlds. This is a clear reference to the Dionysian precedent. We should not be surprised at the many parallels between Jesus and Dionysus. No matter how we try to suppress them, the archetypes that dwell within us all will look for avenues of expression. If we shut the door, they will come in the window. If we force them to take off one disguise, they will reappear in another.

Jesus and Dionysus are both sons of divine fathers and

mortal, virgin mothers. Christ harrowed hell, Dionysus emerged from the underworld. Semele ascended to Olympus as Thyone, the Virgin Mary ascended to heaven. Dionysus and Jesus were both hailed as the King of Kings. At Eleusis the followers of Dionysus celebrated his "Advent" with a newborn baby placed in a winnowing basket—the forerunner of baby Jesus in the manger.

Both Jesus and Dionysus die—Jesus on the cross, Dionysus at the hands of the Titans; and both are reborn, symbolizing the life that does not end. Dionysus ascends to Olympus, Jesus to heaven, and both sit at the right hand of their father.

Like Jesus, Dionysus was usually not believed when he claimed to be the son of God. Both suffered at the hands of local political authorities; both had retinues comprising outcasts and women of questionable repute; and both showed a disregard for the established modes of worship.

And, of course, the wine. One of Jesus' miracles was turning water into wine, something Dionysus can be said to do on a regular basis: One waters the vine, grows the grape, and turns it into wine. Eucharist is a ceremony of *ex stasis*—drinking the wine, the blood of God, and transcending time and space to become for a moment divine.

So we have tried to kill the god, to extinguish the ecstatic experience. But he always returns, and with each return he seems to gain strength and power. We dethrone Dionysus, tear him to bloody bits, boil him in a pot, and he returns as Jesus. We crucify Jesus, and he is reborn.

6. Women and Dionysus: Celebration of Life

Blessed are they who keep the rites of the mother, Cybele!
ANCIENT HYMN TO DIONYSUS FROM EURIPIDES, *THE BACCHAE*

What does the term *Greek god* suggest to you? Most people will think of Apollo—god of light and truth. Blond, bronzed, and made of muscle, he is the prototype of our cartoon super-heroes. The sensuous Dionysus is everything Apollo is not. Born male, Dionysus was raised as a girl by the nymphs. Greek art portrays him sometimes as an old man, most frequently as an effeminate youth. On Olympus he took the seat of the goddess Hestia, both replacing her and carrying on her tradition.

Our society is not comfortable with Dionysian ambiguity. The ancient Greeks, on the other hand, had a fairly relaxed idea about what constituted the proper expression of male sexuality. And so we have another reason for Dionysus's absence from our lives.

Just as we use neckties symbolically to separate our minds from our bodies, we also tend to allocate one set of psychological experiences to men and the other to women. To men we give the head—logic and discrimination, the finding of facts; to women we give the body—emotion, intuition. This is the realm of Dionysus. Perhaps for this reason Dionysus has always been especially beloved by women.

The Maenads

It is ironic that modern women often feel estranged from the ecstatic experience. The original Dionysian worshipers were the Maenads. These wild women of the mountains were the last devotees of the Great Goddess, the ancient matrifocal religion that the new patriarchal order was beginning to replace. They took their god, Dionysus, off into the woods to do their night revelry, the women's mysteries into which Rhea had initiated him. The women's mysteries were always held at night and were so secret, and the secret so well kept, that today we do not really know exactly what went on.

According to Monica Sjöö and Barbara Mor,

> Anthropologist Jacquetta Hawkes . . . believes that the ecstatic mystery religion of Dionysus, the "tender-faced and curly haired" son of the Cretan Great Mother, was originally the cult of the Great Goddess herself, and her wild orgiastic women. . . .
>
> [The Maenads possessed] the magical power to make the earth blossom. Rites were performed on the mountaintops, and at the touch of these wild women's wands . . . streams of wine and water, milk and honey, broke free and flowed from the rocks. in their . . . fury, at the dark of the moon, they would tear any man in pieces who happened to cross their path or enter their sacred precincts. Dionysus himself . . . was torn apart ritually and eaten as a sacrament . . .

Some stories have it that the Maenads were so intoxicated with the joy and ecstasy and abandon of their god Dionysus that finally they tore *him* to pieces and sent him to the underworld, the realm of Hades, where he was fermented as the grape is fermented and he came forth as the wine, his present form.

The Life Force

To worship Dionysus is to worship the life force. The pirates who tried to bind Dionysus—tried in effect to bind the ecstatic principle of organic growth—found they could not do it. Grapevines grew in wild profusion, ivy twined madly, and wine streamed down the deck of the ship. The vibrant energy of the earth inevitably triumphs over human efforts to suppress it, just as a tree's growing roots will eventually burst through a concrete sidewalk that has been laid over them.

As the Greek society and psyche began to move from the emotional, feeling-level female values to the rational masculine world, the old goddesses became less influential. When Hestia stepped down from Olympus to give Dionysus her seat, it signaled a new era. For the Greeks Hestia was the original carrier of the ecstatic principle. Sacrifice to her was an integral part of daily life in ancient Greece. Her household duties of cooking and firing the hearth were invested with the ecstatic experience and the women who carried out these activities in daily life were carrying on the ecstatic principle.

The ancient matrifocal cultures valued the mother above all. Strange through it may seem, for many thousands of years the role of the father in procreation was not understood. It is natural, then, that our ancestors so greatly respected the qualities of the mother—home, birth, growth, nurturing, caring, empathy—and prized them as life sustaining. They nurtured these psychological qualities in themselves, and the sensuous Dionysus was a new twist to a long tradition.

Our society emphasizes the tangible "masculine" values—aggression, power, winning, success, facts, intellectual abilities, concrete proof. The less tangible "feminine" values carry little weight. As a result many women today feel that there is no place for the Dionysian experience in their lives. But they must remember that it was Hestia who was the original ecstatic, and that there is the very essence of ecstatic life of the most ordinary of so-called feminine activities. A woman who cooks for her family sustains their lives. A woman who cleans the home and keeps it safe makes an environment that encourages growth. And in the ultimate female function of giving birth to another human being, a woman ensures the continuance of humankind.

With the exception of giving birth, of course, there is no reason why men cannot and should not also share in the nurturing process and enjoy the sensuous life. And there is no reason why women cannot lead lives of strength and wisdom. This is what it means to touch Dionysus, to feel a part of the ecstatic, creative, and eternal force of life. When we no longer relegate one set of values to men and another to women, when we can be equally male and female, we will touch Dionysus, the divine androgyne.

7. Androgyny: The Union of Male and Female

The anima and animus should function as a bridge, or a door, leading to the images of the collective unconscious, as the persona should be a sort of bridge into the world.

C. G. JUNG

Dionysus is the divine adrogyne, the god who perfectly assimilates male and female. As we learn to recognize the Dionysian archetype in ourselves, we will become more aware and accepting of our own male and female aspects.

The meaning of this psychological androgyny was forcefully brought home to me one day when a friend and I climbed a high mountain in India to see the temple of Gomata (who, in a later incarnation, founded the Jain religion). This great, seventy-foot-high statue, carved of one block of stone, stands at the top of the mountain at the end of an eight-hundred-step ascent. And at his foot—just at the height of the toenail, which is human height—there's a most lovely life-sized statue of a great, buxom-breasted goddess.

I exclaimed to my friend, "What a beautiful goddess!" And he replied with a smile, "I have to inform you that it is a god, not a goddess." Surprised, I said, "Please explain." "Well," he said, "before the fall of man, a baby was nursed by both his father and his mother. This is how a hero was produced."

That's a psychological truth, as true now as it ever was in any time in history. If you want to nurture the heroic side of yourself, you must nurse it with both your masculine and feminine natures. This will produce the Dionysian quality for you.

Anima and Animus

Where do we go to find the repressed Dionysus in ourselves? He lives a hole-and-corner existence, searching out those places where we have only partial or no control. Certainly the realm of anima and animus is one of those. In Jungian terms androgyny is the integration of masculine and feminine "soul images." *Anima*, the feminine, means "soul"; *animus*, the masculine, means "spirit." A man's anima appears in his dreams as a woman; a woman dreams of her animus as a man. Jungian psychology would say that when we dream of the opposite sex, even if that dream image represents a real person, we are actually dreaming of our soul image.

We naturally tend to emphasize the qualities of whatever gender we happen to be. To become psychologically and spiritually unified, however, each of us must make a synthesis of our masculine and feminine qualities. In Jungian terms Dionysus represents perfect psychological harmony. Dionysus is neither a man who dreams of a woman, nor a woman who dreams of a man. He is both: self-nurturing and complete.

We hear a lot about androgyny these days. "The new androgyny" is hailed in the pages of fashion magazines: Girls wear sweatshirts and blue jeans; boys wear pink shirts and earrings. Because we have become more aware of the way our language can stereotype sex roles, mailmen have become mail carriers, firemen have become fire fighters, stewardesses have become flight attendants. Many women are now working at what were formerly considered to be "men's jobs," and more men are staying at home to mind the babies.

Some of us like these moves away from the old roles and stereotypes, and some of us are uncomfortable with them. I think this is because we are dealing with outer change— clothes, names, roles—without having made an inner change to befriend both our male and female aspects.

Without question, men and women are different from one

another. Quite naturally, the two genders express opposite aspects of the human spectrum. Physically, men and women are different. Emotionally and psychologically, there is a wide range. But, to compound the separation, men and women in our society have been raised so differently that we do in fact see different worlds. Most women are raised—subtly or overtly—to please, to serve, to cede their wills; men are raised to initiate, to create, to be boldly decisive, "to go where no man has gone before." We suffer with our stereotypes: Men are "strong," women are "weak"; men are "rational," women are "irrational"; men "bring home the bacon," women cook it. We place these burdens on ourselves and wonder why we can't carry them. We know, consciously or unconsciously, that these labels and expectations are nonsense; but overcoming them is very, very difficult.

Our Judeo-Christian tradition has done a heroic job of preventing the divine androgyny within us from reuniting itself. In Orthodox Judaism, for example, men and women cannot worship together; they must sit in different sections of the temple. Men speak of women, and women of men, as though they were of different species. Women shake their heads and say, "Men. They're all alike." Men respond, "Women. You can't live with 'em and you can't live without 'em." Because we have lost touch with our anima or animus we have lost touch with each other and with the Dionysian principle, which would give us so much of joy and ecstasy if we but knew it.

Male/Female Relationships

In our personal lives we work out anima–animus struggles with our partners. Dionysus is said to be the only god who never quarreled with his wife. Psychologically, he was completely at peace with his male and female aspects.

When we cannot communicate with our inner man or woman, we cannot communicate with the physical men and women with whom we must interact. If you have the objectivity to observe your personal life, you will see that family fights are more in the nature of ritual than they are of any understanding. If you are a participant, of course, the emotion of the moment will blind you to the fact. But if you can stand off just a little way, you will see immediately that arguments and family fights—which are almost exclusively anima–animus tugs of war—accomplish nothing. They never settle anything. Perhaps, at their very best, they discharge some energy; but one has only to fight the battle again as soon as more energy has built up. Poor-quality Dionysus thrives here. To listen to a family quarrel you'd think there was no hope and that the family was doomed. But it usually patches up to fight another day.

Spiritual Mates

Dionysus married Ariadne, the Queen of Athens, who had not had a good marriage to Theseus—in fact, he abandoned her on an island from which Dionysus later saved her. Ariadne then married Dionysus as her second, *spiritual* husband.

Many married women of the time took Dionysus as a second husband. In the Catholic church nuns take Jesus as their spiritual husband. In our own day, in cultures other than our own, shamans often take a human wife as their second wife because they are married to the interior spirit goddess, the anima, as their first wife.

I once heard this very touching tale from a Native American shaman: His intermediary went to a young woman and said, "The shaman wants you for his wife, because he's already married to his spiritual wife. And if you marry him, you're going to have to understand that you'll be his second wife and take a subservient position in that sense."

Many people have a spiritual wife or husband whether they like it or not—and even whether they know it or not. And sometimes their flesh-and-blood wife or husband feels as if she or he takes second place to someone unknown. Quite often they do not understand this at all.

Perhaps the best-known spiritual wife in literature is Dante's Beatrice, his guide through heaven and hell. He was much more married to Beatrice than he was to his real wife, about whom we know so little. Once the wife of a patient came into my office unannounced and took her husband's hour. She said, "I'm serving notice on you that I'm not going to be Beatrice to my husband." She did not want her husband to see her as an ideal woman, she wanted to be appreciated for herself. This situation can be terribly difficult, and underscores our need to know our *own* inner woman or man.

Denial of Pleasure

Anima and animus are powerful psychological forces that can wreak havoc in our lives if lived unconsciously. As an archetype Dionysus, like the soul, is eternal. The body dies, the soul lives on—or, as in many Eastern religions, returns to live another life on earth in its pursuit of wholeness. If we deny Dionysus, we deny our soul; and if we deny our soul, we will become dangerously off balance.

For us, our repression of Dionysus has meant our repression of ecstasy. Our overidentification with mind has made us disrespectful of sensation and intuition. Oriental religions, often thought of as bastions of spirituality, respect the body as a legitimate means of enlightenment. Hatha yoga, Chinese Taoism, Tantric yoga, and others have made a sacrament of the sensuous world as a path to the divine union. In the West, however, much of the Judeo-Christian tradition has done its best to keep earth and heaven from uniting.

When we do honor our physical self it is generally with guilt and anxiety. We feel that we must cover the ecstasy of physical pleasure with alcohol or embarrassment or guilt. As a Frenchman once said of the English, they take their pleasures so gloomily!

The Jewish consciousness in its traditional attitudes never adopted the repression of Dionysus to the extent that our Anglo-Saxon world has done. A Jewish proverb observes that whatever legitimate pleasure we deny ourselves on earth will also be denied us in heaven. When we deny ourselves the Dionysian experience, we also deny ourselves true knowledge of ourselves, our mates, the life process, joy. We deny ourselves heaven on earth.

8. The Return of the Scapegoat

> . . . and Aaron shall lay both his hands upon the head of the live goat, and confess over him all the iniquities of the people of Israel, and all their transgressions, and all their sins; and he shall put them upon the head of the goat, and send him away into the wilderness. . . . The goat shall bear all their iniquities upon him to a solitary land; and he shall let the goat go in the wilderness.
>
> LEVITICUS 16:21–22

In biblical times on Yom Kippur, the Jewish day of atonement, all the sins of the Jewish people were heaped on the back of a goat. The goat was then driven off into the wilderness, ostensibly taking all the evils away with it. To this day we "scapegoat" certain groups of people, conveniently blaming them for all the ills of society.

Somebody—I wish I knew who it was—defined our age as the time when the Old Testament scapegoats are coming home. Leading them is the original scapegoat, Dionysus.

The Goat

The Greeks had a powerful ceremony to ensure the continuance of the ecstatic principle. They took a young goat to symbolize Dionysus, killed it, cut it into seven pieces, and stewed it in its mother's milk. Psychologically, they took the irrational, jumpy quality symbolized by the goat and killed it, returning it to the underworld, taking it back to where it came from. They put the goat into its mother's milk to take it back to its origin, where there is only peace and happiness. They then ate this as a kind of Communion. This was the highest symbol of the ecstatic quality that the Greeks could devise.

The Romans took this ecstatic quality and perverted it by

making Dionysus into Bacchus and crowning him the god of drunkenness. Their culture reveled in materialism and excess, and Dionysus was perverted to their own use.

He fared no better with the Jews, who like the Greeks had lived a matrifocal life for a long time before their recorded history began. Dionysus was no stranger to the Jews. Coins from this time, found near Gaza, picture Dionysus on one side and Jehovah on the other.

At around this time the Jews seem to have decided—at least in their collective unconscious—to establish a patriarchal society based almost exclusively on masculine laws and ruled by the vengeful, judgmental Jehovah. We have the legacy of that decision to this day. Our reasonableness and sense of discipline come largely from the Jewish genius of setting up a patriarchal society. But they could do this only by an almost total suppression of Dionysus, the other side of the coin.

Fortunately, a bit of Dionysus does live on in the Jewish tradition—far more than in the Christian tradition as it is practiced in most of the Western world. As a culture Judaism never lost its spontaneity, love of dance, and humor. But the Jews had so much of this quality that, subconsciously, they felt in danger of being overwhelmed by it. So they put a lid on it. And I think at the high point of Jewish history they struck a beautiful cultural balance—the spark and fun of Dionysus with enough of the patriarchal form for structure. But we in the Western world have forgotten spontaneity and brightness and have taken only Jehovah, the god of vengeance who thunders the law.

The Jews banned the Dionysian quality in a very interesting way. In Leviticus it is said, "It is forbidden to seethe a kid in its mother's milk." This curious injunction was the process of banishing forever the Dionysian quality, which was so strong in the Greek world around them.

In Orthodox Jewish households to this day there are two sets of cooking utensils—one for meat and one for dairy. Anything that is cooked with meat is served on one set of dishes, eaten with its own utensils, and washed in its own dishpan.

The same goes for the dairy food. In this way the kid may never meet its mother's milk again. The Dionysian quality is banished.

This enormous effort on the part of the Jews to maintain their identity in a world largely fashioned by Greek thought still has an effect on us today, because of course we follow the Judeo-Christian tradition and have the Old Testament qualities about us. Thus the Dionysian in us has been officially obliterated.

The Sheep

The goat was now off-limits. So what did Judaism and, later, Christianity do for a symbol? It adopted the sheep, "the Lamb of God who taketh away our sins": about as opposite a symbol as one could devise.

The sheep is certainly not like the mischievous goat. It is docile, the eternal victim. The Bible refers many times to the sheep being separated from the goats. We have translated this in our modern Western minds as separating the right from the wrong, the noble from the ignoble, the righteous from the unrighteous. That mythology has been built into us so deeply that the goat quality, the ecstatic Dionysian quality, still does not function in us today.

Sheep represent everything of value in our Judeo-Christian world. The sheep, in fact, is the chief determinant of our currency. Every currency in the Western world—the shilling, the franc, the deutsche mark, the lira, the peso, and the Austrian thaller (from which we get our dollar)—was the price of one sheep. For centuries there was no inflation in the Western world because one of our money pieces was worth a sheep. You could count on that anywhere, anytime.

The Scapegoat

So the sheep was in and the goat, Dionysus, was out totally. The ecstatic quality, the capriciousness of life that the Greeks enjoyed so much, was discredited. The goat became the scape-goat. It was given a very bad name—so bad that it came to represent the worst evil. Dionysus Melangius, "Dionysus of the Black Goatskin," was an ancient scapegoat-satyr form of the god, whose appearance greatly influenced the medieval Christian notion of what the devil should look like. To this day the devil is pictured with the goat's horns, cloven hooves, and tail. In medieval Christian Europe, goats were renowned for their lechery and were said to be familiars of witches.

Significantly, the scapegoated groups are usually those that are out of power. The classic example of this in our own time is the scapegoating of the Jews by the Nazis in the 1930s and 1940s. In the West the decision makers are typically adult, white, Anglo-Saxon males who hold responsible positions. Our scapegoats, then, are the ones who do not fit the mold—women, people of color or other religions, youth, artists. To these groups we give the attributes of Dionysus. Women are often said to be irrational, unpredictable, capricious, and likely to turn violent, especially sexually: "Hell hath no fury like a woman scorned." (Remember Hera?) The stereotypical black or Latino is thought of as "naturally musical." Such groups are "not to be trusted" with rational decisions. And the youth, of course, are considered to be hopeless. Their music screams, their dancing is wild, and they are completely unpredictable.

Return of the Scapegoat

What happens to a scapegoat? Does it disappear, never to be seen again? Absolutely not. Scapegoats will eventually return to those who sent them away.

Our scapegoats are coming home, and leading them is Dionysus—emerging once again from the sea of the collective unconscious, reborn in our world and asking to be humanized before his archetypal energy runs amok. As he did in ancient times, the god is throwing off his chains, flowing as glorious wine, and demanding to be heard.

And he will be heard, because this is the inescapable truth: You cannot kill a god. You can only repress him, sacrifice him, drive him to the underworld and to a new epiphany. But you cannot get rid of him. We carry the archetype of ecstasy deep within us, and it must be lived out with dignity and consciousness. The scapegoat, Dionysus, is returning; and we must recognize him and welcome him back gladly.

9. Filled with Light or Filled with Air?

What an opening! A 12-foot spacewalking astronaut, a spaceship and a blimp flew over the crowd on guy-wires. There were flashing spotlights, exploding flashpots, belching fog everywhere, deafening noise for four minutes. . . . Thousands of boys and young men. . . . pushed, shoved, slam-danced and reached riot-pitch as the band increased its sonic attack. . . . At the show's climax . . . a gargantuan inflatable head . . . billowed up under Nicko McBrain's drum kit at stage center, leaving McBrain bobbing 15 feet above the stage atop the head.

REVIEW OF THE HEAVY METAL BAND IRON MAIDEN
BY LARRY KELP, *OAKLAND TRIBUNE*, FEBRUARY 23, 1987

What goes up must come down.

ANONYMOUS

When Semele became filled with the joyous light of Zeus, she conceived Dionysus. But when she asked the impossible—to look directly at the divine fire—she was destroyed. In the life and death of Semele we can see the positive and negative sides of Dionysian energy: enthusiasm and inflation.

Enthusiasm and Inflation

Enthusiasm is truly a divine word because it means "to be filled with God" (*en-theo-ism*). Thus to be visited by an enthusiasm is legitimately to be filled with God. The soul is enhanced where the self is activated—a beautiful experience. Joy is a part of this.

Inflation, on the other hand (and this is a meaning that Jung attached to this word), means to be filled with air—generally hot air. Inflation means to be blown up, to have your ego puffed up, to be arrogant. It is always an egocentric experience because one has taken the air, the spirit, and assimilated it with the ego—and then one goes off like the puffed-up idiot that one has become.

We must know the difference between an enthusiasm, which is entirely legitimate—a visitation of God—and an inflation, which is always followed by a crash of some kind. If you find that you can't stop a flow of energy, then—paradoxically— you *must* stop it. If you can't put on the brakes and slow down, then do anything—bail out, jump off—but do whatever you have to do to stop. Because that which takes on a life and momentum of its own and can't be stopped *must* be stopped, and as quickly as possible. This is a good test for inflation.

An inflation is always of traumatic proportions; in fact, it is a small psychosis. We go a little mad, get driven out of our true orbit, and become a fanatic.

Certainly none of us is immune to inflation—myself included. I will never forget the Englishman in London who, after quietly listening to me hold forth on some of my youthful carryings on, leveled a very steady finger at me and said,"You, sir, are a heretic and a fanatic." I was deflated on the spot, and I have never been so subject to fanaticism again. He woke me up.

Induction and conduction, a pair of terms from the language of electricity, can help explain how enthusiasm and inflation work. Induction is characteristic of enthusiasm. You stand close enough to a source of energy to be energized or warmed or quickened by it, but none of that energy flows into your system directly. For example, you can safely warm yourself by standing near a radiator. Conduction, in contrast, consists of direct contact with a source of energy. Some of that energy comes flooding into you directly—just as if you put your finger into a light socket.

All transformers work on the principle of induction. Electricity of proper voltage goes through a coil and back out where it came from. Other coils, very close by, get a charge of energy excited by induction and take their energy off for household use—lower voltage, generally. But no energy from the first set ever enters directly into the second set.

This is excellent; this is safe, controllable transformation of energy. Semele was able to be impregnated by Zeus because he appeared to her transformed; she received the god by induction. In this way we can stand close to God or to the collective unconscious and be safe. When 100,000 volts of unconscious energy flows on its way, 110-volt household current is generated in our human lives, and we are enlightened by it.

But should conduction begin, then some of that 100,000 volts would leap directly over to the second system and blow it up. It would be as if 100,000 volts suddenly began to flow into your wall sockets. It would break everything! It is no wonder that when Semele looked directly into the fiery face of Zeus, god of the thunderbolt, she was incinerated.

So: Induction produces enthusiasm and conduction produces inflation. These are good models to go by.

Inflation: Put on the Brakes

Inflation, the conduction, makes us behave as if we were mad. This is such a wretched business because it is like drunkenness—Dionysus in his degraded, Bacchanalian form. When you get drunk the first thing you lose is your capacity to see that you are getting drunk.

The first inkling I have that I'm inflating doesn't come from me, because at that point it's already too late—I'm too pleased with myself to have any objectivity. So how do I know? If I am giving a lecture I hear a wretched tone of voice echoing off the back wall. I hear this high-pitched whine, a wail, and I know that I've gone off into inflation—something that everyone who has been listening to me has been painfully aware of for the last half-hour. So when I hear this tone I simply stop speaking, take a deep breath, and continue in a more human manner.

For many of us, unfortunately, inflation has become the

norm. A thing must be outsized if it is to interest us. Car dealers try to sell us "the deal of the century"; we have to work our way through a forest of neon signs, desperately flashing their messages to get our attention, just to walk down the street; fast-food restaurants have no small-size order of fries, just "regular" and "large." We moderns are so jaded, for any of a hundred different reasons, that unless we are inflated we feel that there's no life going on. We must go out and squeal the tires, blast our eardrums with sound.

We are so inured to the things of the spirit that we actively search for the inflation rather than for the enthusiasm. And because Dionysus is served up to us so often in the form of inflation—dancing nude on the beach, participating in group sex, getting roaring drunk and tearing up the town—he has gotten a very bad name. This is the hardest struggle in discussing Dionysus: the fact that almost all the examples of him are issuing forth into the world as inflation and are destructive.

The negative Dionysus has perhaps nowhere been as destructive as it was when expressed as the Nazism of the 1930s and 1940s in Germany, which scapegoated the Jews so terribly. It was made up of legitimate material that came flooding up from the German unconscious. But it affixed itself to the collective German ego to become one of the worst fanaticisms and inflations that the world has ever known. And what wreckage it left in its wake!

The details of the rise of Nazism are extremely interesting. Dr. Jung said that he felt something brewing in the German psyche soon after World War I. He wrote his first article about it in 1921, and spoke of the blond beast stirring in the German unconscious. The beast surfaced as Nazism in the early 1930s and came forth as World War II, a whirlwind that devastated Europe. What a lesson to learn! Jung felt that it was Wotan, the German Dionysus, who had energized and fueled the Nazi movement. Wotan was called the Berserker, a word which has been drawn into the English language to mean "that which has run amok."

For centuries it had been foretold in Europe that the Third

Reich would rise in Europe and be its salvation. Jung, of course, knew about this; and when Nazism first came rushing out of the German unconscious and was labeled the Third Reich, he was cautiously interested. He watched and waited, looked and wondered. Was this the heralded Wotan, rushing up to illuminate twentieth-century Europe?

One day in Germany Jung had occasion to go to a Hitler rally and hear the führer speak. All Jung's hopes were dashed. "It is madness," he said, and immediately began to write against it. He became so vocal that before the end of the war the Nazis had put a price on Jung's head.

Enthusiasm!

When we see frightening examples of negative Dionysian energy, such as Nazism, we are rightfully afraid of doing any work with the Dionysian quality in ourselves. We say, "He's too dangerous. He drives people to do crazy things." This is a bit like saying that you should never go to a hospital because people so often die there. The argument is compelling but it doesn't hold up. If we understand the difference between enthusiasm, being filled with God, and inflation, being filled with hot air, we will be quite safe.

So how can we—safely—invite Dionysus back into our lives? With enthusiasm! To express ecstasy with dignity and consciousness we must meet it head on, with a joyful spirit of acceptance

Enthusiasm annuls the distance between the pairs of opposites, and this brings ecstatic joy. A visitation of God, which enthusiasm gives, transcends the duality of one's life—the either/or—and brings them into a synthesis. This is an experience beyond price. Then, for a short time—because this is all that we can stand—the opposites cease torturing us. When we transcend the cross of opposites, we will find ecstatic joy.

10. The God Connection

You do not have an inferior function, it has you.

C. G. JUNG

Pentheus, Lycurgus, the crew of the pirate ship—none of them could control Dionysus. The flow of life cannot be bound by ropes or rules. In the same way, we cannot ultimately control or deny within ourselves the inherent freedom of this ecstatic archetype. It will always burst forth: This is its nature.

We must seek, then, not to refuse the ecstatic experience but to welcome it. We may be uneasy about this welcome, because we are inviting something we do not fully comprehend and over which we have the least control. This part of us that is least in control Jung calls the *inferior function*, and it is here we will finally contact our untapped Dionysian energy.

The Four Functions

We have spoken throughout this book of the realms of thinking and feeling, sensation and intuition. Now it is time to explore these terms in more depth and see how they relate to the Dionysian experience.

According to Jungian psychology the human personality has four aspects, or *functions*, set in two opposing pairs. The first pair is *thinking* and *feeling;* the second pair is *intuition* and *sensation*. The first pair is rational, the second irrational.

Thinking concerns rational intellectual functioning, what we think about things. Feeling has to do with our values, how we feel emotionally about a situation. Intuition implies a nonverbal, irrational perception of ideas, outcomes, and situations. Sensation has to do with nonrational, sensate perception of the physical world of objects—their sizes, shapes, colors, smells, sounds. Jung explained the four functions in this way:

The essential function of sensation is to establish that something exists, thinking tells us what it means, feeling what its value is, and intuition surmises whence it comes and goes. Sensation and intuition I call irrational functions, because they are both concerned simply with what happens and with actual or potential realities. Thinking and feeling, being discriminatory functions, are rational. Sensation . . . rules out simultaneous intuitive activity, since the later is not concerned with the present but is rather a sixth sense for hidden possibilities, and therefore should not allow itself to be unduly influenced by existing reality. In the same way, thinking is opposed to feeling, because thinking should not be influenced or deflected from its purpose by feeling values, just as feeling is vitiated by too much reflection.

Very early in life we get the first function going—just the first small beginnings of consciousness. When the first function is established, a second function is added. In our culture this happens around early adolescence. Then, when we can stand it, a third function is added. And that brings us to the ordinary, everyday kind of consciousness in which most of us live.

We each "specialize" in one function, the one that comes most naturally. This is called our *superior function*. The opposing one of the pair, that which is least in our control, is called our *inferior function*. (This is a greatly simplified explanation. It is important to remember that no one exemplifies these functions as clearly in real life as it is possible to do in theory.) Each of us has all the aspects to some degree, and through their complex interplay we each express our unique personality.

Which Is My Inferior Function?

It is tempting to make the model continue in an orderly fashion and think that our fourth function, the inferior function, will soon turn up and everything will be just fine. Theoretically, if all four functions were conscious, one would be an enlightened being. But as much as we would like this to happen, it rarely does. I often hear people who are familiar with the system say, "I'm working on my fourth function. I've almost got it now." Unfortunately, no such thing happens. We do not get functions one, two, three, and four in on orderly manner. The advent of the fourth function is usually a total disaster—at least from the standpoint of the ego, whose very existence seems to be threatened.

The fourth function is the representation of the unlived life we still contain. Because we have never dealt with it head on, when it comes rushing in, it naturally scares us out of our wits! We feel totally at sea. Our ego is no longer running the show, and we no longer have the modicum of control for standard behavior that we thought we had when only the three functions were conscious. Usually this happens around the age of forty-five, but most people delay it considerably past that—it takes a lot of maturity and experience to handle the sudden appearance of the wholeness in oneself.

The natural question at this point is, "How can I tell which is my inferior function?" I am sorry to tell you that in answer to this question Dr. Jung once replied, "How can you find a lion who has just swallowed you?"

The chief characteristic of the inferior function is that it is out of control. Because we have not lived it very much, it still contains all its primal energy. When we have drained away much of its energy, the superior function grows thin and is no longer adequate. Then the inferior function, with all of its unlived energy, comes rushing up.

We usually specialize in one of the four qualities. We will

probably make our living with it, and may even be well known for it. If you have a superior *sensation* function, you are at ease with the physical world. You know the size, shape, color, texture, and location of the objects and beings around you without having to think about them consciously. Intuition, then, is your inferior function. You are most comfortable with concrete explanations. You may have a terribly difficult time handling the unknown, populating the future with the out-of-control figures of your intuition.

Any repressed material in our personalities automatically begins to revolve around our inferior functions. For example, let's look at the thinking type. Most people will understand this type, because it is the dominant one in our fact-oriented society. *Thinking* types make informed opinions about situations—good or bad, right or wrong. If you are a thinking type, when you toss and turn at three in the morning you're subjected to your inferior function, which is feeling. The whole orgiastic, out-of-control, vague-yearnings-for-tropical-paradise quality comes rushing up by way of your inferior function.

Feeling types have rational perceptions on the emotional level and will judge things comfortable or uncomfortable, wonderful or awful, according to how they feel at the moment. If you are a feeling type you probably torture yourself with an orgy of poor-quality thinking in Dionysian form. You may construct utopias and gardens of Eden three times a week—but they come down as easily as they go up!

Intuitive types perceive the total situation nonrationally—its background, present, and likely outcome. They do this without consciously thinking about it. If you are intuitive you form general impressions, abstract ideas, rather than concrete detail, and you will have sensation as your inferior function. I once knew an architect who was wonderfully intuitive. Unfortunately, this led him to build an absolutely beautiful bookstore with curved walls in which no bookshelves could ever be satisfactorily installed. Don't ever try to earn your living with your inferior function!

The Inferior Function Under Pressure

You may tax your superior function to the limit, and it will always see you through. But you must protect your inferior function at all costs, because it goes wild under pressure. Let me give you an example.

I went out with a friend of mine, a solid sensation type, to help him buy his first car. My inferior function is thinking—thinking, in fact, is a nightmare for me. What looks like thinking is intuition sort of pulled over the void to cover up the hole. This seems to work pretty well, and I've produced reasonably good products. But it's not thinking in the sense that it would be if thinking were a conscious faculty.

So there we were, looking for a car. Two more dissimilar people I could hardly imagine! I was busy with my intuitive and feeling faculty and I said, "Well, let's see. Now we'll go to a car dealer and find out what a new car costs, then we'll go look in the newspaper for ads, then we'll watch on the street as cars go by, then we'll have to decide whether we have to buy new snow tires or wait until fall . . . " And I was in the middle of all this when I heard my friend moan with despair. "Robert, stop! I can't stand it! We're going to the Volkswagen dealer and we're going to buy a car, and not one more word out of you!"

All these possibilities bubbling out of my intuition just floored him. He couldn't stand it. So we went straight to the Volkswagen dealer, and I didn't say a word about any other kind of car, or about snow tires. He drove the car home and he wouldn't speak to me for twenty-four hours. These are signs of the inferior function being overtaxed. Yet it is precisely from this rubbed-raw, vulnerable part of oneself that the splendor of God will find its way to you.

The God Connection

Carl Jung says that the inferior function is always one's God connection. He can come no other way. We have him effectively barred on every other front, but we can't keep him out through the inferior function because we have no control there. It is as though we were keeping a bull in a pen of which we owned only three sides. We keep those three sides in good repair, with the gate always locked securely. But the fourth side is owned by a neighbor who doesn't care about the bull and never keeps the fence up. Because we have no control over this side of the fence this is the hole through which the bull will come rushing out.

Like the bull, the inferior function will come rushing out. Unlike the bull, however, we do not have to run away from it. The point is *not* to run away from our inferior function. We must work with it and endure it if we are to retrieve the Dionysian quality of ecstasy that lies within it.

Suppose you have intuition as your superior function. You work well with ideas, abstractions, airy thoughts, possibilities. Sensation, then, is your inferior function. You have two left feet and any number of thumbs when you enter the world of sensate things and mechanics. If you want to engage your inferior function you might spend a Saturday afternoon building a birdhouse in your backyard—a project which will undoubtedly involve at least one mashed thumb, several bandages, and a product of doubtful quality. But the exposure to your inferior function will awaken in you a kind of ecstatic quality you rarely encounter in the more usual departments of your life. It is in such things that the Dionysian faculty makes itself known.

The inferior function frequently has a compulsive quality about it. When we engage in fanaticism, or find it necessary to put extra vehemence into an argument, or find ourselves doing or saying things we know to be destructive, then we are off into a dangerous inflation. We are experiencing the compulsive nature of the inferior function.

This is acutely painful, but it is precisely here that we can reclaim the Dionysian spirit if we will do the inner work required to bring this element into relationship with our better-differentiated faculties. What good could come out of Nazareth? The best and highest good. In the same way our best spiritual development can come from our most inferior nature.

How Dionysus Enters Through the Inferior Function: A Dream

I once had a dream of great impact that illustrates the way in which Dionysus enters through the inferior function. Here is my dream:

A boy had been drowned in a river and we were to recover his dead body. We were instructed to find him using only our feet. We could not use our hands or any other faculties. I waded out as far as I could go, but I could not find the body with my feet. Finally, I tilted my head back so that I could go just a little deeper, and I stumbled right onto the dead body. With some maneuvering, and without using my hands, I got the drowned body out of the river, into the house, and onto the bed. Then, for the first time, I saw that the boy emitted a light, as if he had a halo around his body. To our astonishment the boy sat up and began speaking words of great wisdom. At that moment someone whispered, "Here comes his mother. This is going to be harder on her than finding him dead."

This dream speaks directly of my inferior function. It is represented by my feet, the lowest part of my body. This is the only faculty through which I can restore that lost part of my personality represented by the drowned boy. It was probably about the age of the drowned boy that I lost touch with my own Dionysian world through the training I was subjected to from my fundamentalist Anglo-Saxon environment. Only through my inferior function could I recover the boy, bring him into consciousness, and rediscover the radiant and winsome quality that he represents. The closing words hint that this can be done only at the expense of the mother complex, the wish to return to childhood, in myself.

Some years later I discovered another level of meaning in this dream. In Christian symbolism it is officially possible to enter a Gothic church only through one of the west doors, under one of the two spires. The choir has no doors, although the north and south transepts do. But none of these may be used for official entry. Why? The Gothic church represents the body of Christ. His head is the choir, his arms are the transepts, the crossing in his navel, and the west towers are his feet. It is only through the feet that the heavenly element may enter the body—never, never through the choir, his head. For this reason the bottoms of the feet are called the soles, or "souls," of the feet—it is through this part of the body that the soul enters or leaves. This is yet another eloquent observation that it is only by way of our inferior function that the heavenly element can enter. There is no other way.

When you consciously invite Dionysus in through your inferior function, with your conscious ego as welcoming host, you will begin to experience new and vivid insights you never believed possible. In the next part of this book we shall learn some psychological ways to help us do this.

PART II

TOUCHING ECSTASY

Touching Ecstasy

For a long time now we have lived with the Lamb of God, who taketh away the sins of the world, and a high and beautiful and finely differentiated culture has been won in that fashion. But now it is time to do something for the goat, the joyous Dionysian quality.

It is no longer a question of either/or, the lamb or the goat; we must bring the lamb and the goat together. To do this we must honor both the rational and irrational aspects of ourselves, just as the Greeks once accorded equal honor to Apollo and Dionysus at Delphi.

Unlike the Greeks, however, we have no established Dionysian cult or ritual to which we can turn. We are not likely to tear a goat to pieces these days! Because we have so effectively removed the Dionysian experience from our world, we can no longer look for it outside ourselves. Instead we must turn inward to find the archetype of ecstasy.

We can touch Dionysus and learn to express that archetypal joy through three psychological disciplines: active imagination, dreamwork, and ritual. The first two are wonderful and direct ways to contact the ecstasy and joy within us, and it is in this context that we will discuss them here.* The third, ritual, has been very much neglected in the twentieth century. With it we can learn how to contact the Dionysian element within ourselves, and to contain and formalize the ecstatic experience.

---

* If you would like more information about active imagination and dreamwork, please see my book *Inner Work* (San Francisco: Harper & Row, 1986), which describes these techniques in detail.

Before We Begin

We like to think of ourselves as individuals. But it is important to remember that, on a deep level, we are really plural beings. That is, we are one being made up of quite a number of distinct personalities, behaviors, archetypes, all looking for expression. When we first dip beneath the surface in search of these personalities, we may feel insecure because we are in uncharted waters. For this reason the first appearance of the god can be terrifying, and your first response may be to run for your life.

Don't! Remember, everything comes from one source, and the unity of that oneness can be restored. As I have said elsewhere, a good place to begin our understanding of inner work is with the Nicene Creed, *Credo In Unum Deum:* I believe in one God. Psychologically, this means that there is only one source, one beginning, one unity, out of which all life flows and to which it returns. You cannot get lost because you are already home.

According to Jung, humanity holds a special role in creation: to contribute to the act of consciousness, and the point of view of morality, in its highest sense. Raw archetypes, like tornadoes, are amoral. A tornado doesn't care where it touches down or what it destroys; it is simply acting as it is meant to act. We have no control over the actions of a tornado. We can, however, come to terms with an archetype—because, in a real sense, it is us.

Always remember that you have influence in the archetypal world. In the introduction I told you about Dr. Jung's observation that the ego has the same relationship to the collective unconscious as a cork does to the ocean on which it floats. But because the ego has consciousness, it can make a dialogue of equals with the unconscious. In the same way the "I" and Dionysus are equals; but the "I" has the inestimable value of being conscious. Because both the "I" and the archetype arise from the same source, the collective unconscious, they can find a common ground and strike a common chord.

With this in mind, let us look for Dionysus.

11. Active Imagination: Meeting the Archetype

Now then, who are you and where are you from?

PENTHEUS TO DIONYSUS,
EURIPIDES, *THE BACCHAE*

Active imagination,* a technique developed by Carl Jung some decades ago, is a wonderful way to enter into the mythic reality while still maintaining ordinary reality. In active imagination you can enter into a conversation with the different parts of yourself that live in your unconscious—in this instance, Dionysus. "In this way," as Jung said, "we find that thoughts, feelings, and affects are alive in us which we would never have believed possible."

The level of imagination is such an excellent place to work because it *is* the place of Dionysus. Dionysus, ecstasy, swings between two worlds, transcending both. The imagination is neither the conscious nor the unconscious, but rather what lies between the two. Here, on the meeting ground of imagination, the ego and the archetype can speak as equals, each learning from the other.

You may find it difficult to begin to do active imagination unless you already had some experience with it or with similar techniques. Remember, however, that it is a powerful tool; for those who are unused to it the flow of images can be startling. Therefore I would like to repeat a caution from *Inner Work:*

---

* My book *Inner Work* (San Francisco: Harper & Row, 1986) explores the technique of active imagination in depth. This is an enormous subject, and I cannot begin to do it justice within the constraints of this short book. I advise you to study the instructions in *Inner Work* carefully if you plan to use this pathway.

Before starting active imagination be sure that there is someone available for you to call in case you become overwhelmed by the imagination.

How To Begin

Active imagination does not consist of "making things up." You simply allow information that you already possess, but of which you have no conscious awareness, to come to the surface. Active imagination has some similarity to dreaming, in that you do not censor the flow of images; but during active imagination you are fully awake. Also, as the name implies, it is not passive fantasy. You do not watch an inner drama as you would watch a movie; rather, you become an actor in the drama. Your conscious ego actively engages in conversation with the symbolic images thrown up by your imagination.

You will need a quiet, private place where you can be alone without interruption. You cannot make a dialogue with the psychological images if the day-to-day world is constantly intruding.

Next you must decide on a method to record your dialogue. It is very important to keep a record of this inner work, because afterward it may be difficult to remember details. You may want to use a pencil and paper or, if you find it more convenient, a typewriter or word processor. You may decide to draw or paint what you find.

Now make yourself comfortable. Empty your ego-mind of expectation, and let the images flow. Do not censor them and do not be afraid.

It is important to let the images speak for themselves. After all, they come from you. You should not find yourself putting words in their mouths or directing the flow of conversation. Be interested in what they have to say. If you relax and keep an open mind, the images of your active imagination will communicate effortlessly.

If you are confused by something an image says, ask it for

clarification. You will find that your unconscious mind has answers to the questions your conscious mind has been pondering, just as we often find a dream has solved a difficult problem for us overnight. When your conscious mind absorbs this knowledge from the unconscious, the relationship between the two will change. You will have set up a basis for communication that will lead you to wholeness.

A Sample Dialogue

Let's look at an example of a dialogue in active imagination. This woman recorded her dialogue on a typewriter as it occurred. She designated Dionysus as D and herself as I:

I: [*I see a golden young man sitting on a rock at the edge of a forest.*] Hello, Dionysus. Why is it so difficult to find you?

D: I don't know. I'm right here.

I: Where is that?

D: Inside you. Can't you see me now?

I: Yes, but I've never talked to you before.

D: No, but only because you've never asked. I am always here. [*He smiles.*]

I: I need to know how I can bring the ecstatic quality into my life, but I don't want it to take over. What can I do?

D: You need to get to know me better. I'm not as bad as I'm made out to be.

I: No? Tell me some good things about yourself.

D: Well, I like to paint and draw, and poetry is very important to me. [*He smiles more broadly. He is very, very happy. Golden light radiates from his head.*]

I: I had no idea you were so close. I see you very vividly.

D: Yes, isn't it amazing [*his tone is very dry*]. We gods just go on and on as if we were always here. . . .

I: You have an interesting sense of humor.

D: Yes, I know. [*He begins to laugh.*]

I: So tell me, what can I do to express you?

D: Well, you could tell me a good joke. That would make me happy. I like to be happy above all else.

I: What else could I do?

D: You could run, jump in the air with your hands raised to the sky, twirl around, and think of me. You can yell as loudly as you can. You can feel my energy flowing through your body. You can do this at night, or during the day. Why don't you do it right now and get back to me?

I: OK. [*I get up from my typewriter and do as he instructs.*]

D: That was great. How do you feel?

I: I can't stop smiling. This is wonderful! Thanks.

D: No problem. [*He looks like he knows a lot more than he's saying.*]

I: What else did you want to say?

D: You shouldn't censor me as much as you do. I love you and I'm here to help you. I'm a very important part of your life, and when you shut me out you shut out the world. I'm sitting here at the edge of a beautiful forest. I can take you through the forest and show you its wonders, and I can lead you out again and show you the way around fear. When I am with you, you have no fear. You have fear only when you do not see me.

I: Yes. When I look at you I see that. I feel full of joy and energized.

D: You can come talk to me whenever you like. Let me know when you want to walk in the forest. I am really quite a good and gentle guide. I promise you will come out of the other end of the forest in one piece.

I: Thanks. Well, I've got ten minutes. Is that enough time?

D: Sure. Go ahead.

I: [*We go into the forest. I see some big, white, soft flowers that seem to smile at me and say, "We're all here in the same forest. Peace be with you. We are protecting you." We walk on. Dionysus is smiling gently. He is very firm. He knows exactly where we are going. He holds the back of my neck gently with his hand, and I can feel his energy going up and down my spine.*]

D: Look at that tree.

I: What tree?

D: Over there, the tallest tree in the forest.

I: [*I look up and see a very tall tree. At the top of the tree is a monkey.*] What is that?

D: That is you.

I: Why?

D: Because you can swing from branch to branch as easily as that monkey. You can jump from tree to tree and branch to branch. You can climb as quickly as you can to the top, and scamper down again without falling. You cannot get hurt. Just enjoy yourself. Be filled with joy; there is no room for fear. You can do anything, but you must first *believe* that you can do anything. Remember this monkey and take it with you.

I: Thanks. I certainly wasn't expecting that.

D: No, of course not. I am the unexpected. But, as you see, I am also very familiar. Because I am you.

I: This is a lot for me to absorb.

D: OK, I know. Let's just walk slowly out of the woods and admire the flowers.

I: [*We do. I see small white flowers with shiny green leaves. They are vibrant with energy. They seem to wave good-bye and invite me back. The world here seems infused with a strong, golden, joyous feeling that vibrates through everything.*] Good-bye. thanks for the walk. [*We are now on the other side of the forest.*]

D: That's fine. I'll be here whenever you like. This is where I live.

I: OK, thank you.

D: You're welcome.

Now what has happened here? First, the woman treated the god with courtesy and was treated courteously in return. she made the first greeting and established contact. During the course of the dialogue she also treated her ego with respect— she expressed her fears, made her needs known, and set limits. At the end she thanked Dionysus and established the basis for a possible return visit.

The woman who wrote this had intuition as her superior function. She had previously worked with active imagination and was able to enter into the experience without any problems. Even so, she was surprised by a number of things that happened. She was most surprised by the feeling level of the image, the vibrant energy and joy that were a constant presence during the dialogue and which remained with her for the rest of the day. She was also surprised by the symbolic monkey, and the relation of Dionysus to fear.

Several striking mythic and spiritual motifs were involved in her active imagination. In fact, this experience contains many elements of a shamanic journey. (Shamanism, a part of many ancient cultures, is an ecstatic religion. The spiritual journey of the shaman is intended to heal the human spirit and bring wholeness. To do this the shaman learns to live in both worlds, just as Dionysus bridges both worlds.) This woman was given a ritual to perform which would put her in contact with the Dionysus quality. She was then led on a journey by an image, Dionysus, that established itself as a spirit guide. Finally, she was given an animal "ally," the monkey. By taking on the qualities of the monkey she could learn to conquer physical fear—represented by learning to scamper up and down tall, precariously swaying trees—and experience new power. Because her inferior function is sensation, her fear is in the realm of the physical. It is interesting to note that it was precisely in the place where she had the least control that Dionysus chose to work.

Finally, the experience transformed Dionysus from an abstract concept into a real experience that she can call upon whenever she feels the need. In this way she met the archetype, established a relationship, and gained a nonrational understanding of the quality of ecstasy. Now she can consciously begin to live this quality.

To give a sterner example of active imagination, we can look at the initiation of an Eskimo shaman: The spirit world chooses a youth who is to be a shaman. He is abducted by the spirits and taken to the underworld, where many demons come to eat the flesh off his bones. Finally, he is dismembered and every bone is set apart from every other bone. After a time the spirits come and put him back together again. Great care must be used at this point, because any bone that is left out will be missing for the rest of the shaman's life. New flesh is given to the initiate and he returns to the living world. He is then a shaman and has the power to heal any illness caused by any demon which has eaten his flesh during the initiation. He has no power over an illness caused by a demon which did not take part in his dismemberment.

Each person who engages in active imagination dialogue with Dionysus will see images and have experiences that fit the needs of his or her personality. Though each dialogue is unique to the individual, the inner lessons—which spring from the collective unconscious—are surprisingly similar. Don't prejudge the experience. Keep an open mind and see what happens. You will certainly be surprised!

12. Dreamwork: Working with the Archetype

How often does a man say as he wakes in the morning, "I had a wonderful dream last night," and relate how Mercury or this or that philosopher appeared to him in person and taught him this or that art. But then the dream escapes him and he cannot remember it. However, anyone to whom this happens should not leave his room upon awakening, should speak to no one, but remain alone and sober until everything comes back to him, and he recalls his dream.

PARACELSUS

We all dream. Short of refusing to remember, we can't refuse our dreams or hide from them. They simply reflect what is. Dionysus may naturally appear to us in our dreams. Meeting him on this ground and acting intelligently on the encounter is a fruitful avenue to explore.

Working with Dreams

Dream interpretation is a complex subject about which volumes have been written, and about which few people agree. In the end your dreams will mean something to *you*. And because they are *your* dreams, *your* interpretation is most important. This short chapter cannot begin to cover techniques of dream interpretation and dreamwork, nor should you expect to be able to plunge into dreamwork after you have read it. It will, however, give you some idea of how to connect with your inner Dionysian quality in the framework of dreaming. For more details please see *Inner Work*.

The world we find in dreams is at once strange and familiar.

One reason for this is that our dreams are peopled by archetypes. These prototypes of inner dynamics are outside of time and space; they act and react in an infinite number of ways that would be impossible in real time. These images use the language of symbols, a very deep level of communication. If we are to comprehend the dream, we must look for meaning in this inner level.

Your dream is a great principle laid out for you to study and understand. Watch your dreams carefully, for they will give you an accurate illustration of what is happening in your inner life, what to do about it, and what you can expect from your actions.

When you work with your dreams, try to follow these four basic steps (they are outlined in more detail in *Inner Work*):

1. *Make associations.* What meanings can you give the images in your dreams?
2. *Connect dream images to inner dynamics.* What emotional or spiritual parts of yourself do the dream images represent?
3. *Interpret.* Put together steps 1 and 2 to arrive at the dream's meaning for you.
4. *Ritualize the dream to give it reality.* We will speak about this in more detail in chapter 13.

Two Dreams

By way of illustration I would like to share with you two dreams of my own. They show the transformation of the Dionysian quality over thirty-five years. The first dream is a great archetypal dream. It came to me at the age of twenty-five, when I was a callow youth and very ill-equipped to handle it. Unfortunately, dreams don't always time themselves to one's liking! Here is my dream:

Every thousand years a Buddha is born. In my dream the Buddha is born in the middle of the night. A star shines in the sky to herald the birth of the Buddha. I am there, and I am the same age throughout the dream.

I watch the birth of the Buddha, and I see the Buddha grow up. He is a young man, like me, and we are constant companions. We are happy with each other, and there is much companionship and brightness.

One day we come to the river, which flows in two directions at once. Half the river flows one way, and half flows the other way; where the two streams touch in the center of the river there are very large whirlpools. I swim across, but the Buddha is caught in a whirlpool and drowns.

I am inconsolable; my companion is gone. So I wait a thousand years, a star shines in the night sky again, and again the Buddha is born in the middle of the night. I spend another long period as the companion of the Buddha.

Here the details are lost, but for some reason I have to wait another thousand years for the birth of the third Buddha. Again a star shines, and the Buddha is born in the middle of the night, and I am his companion as he grows up. We're friends and I'm happy. Then I have to wait a thousand years again, till modern times, for the Buddha to be born a fourth time.

This time, however, the circumstances are different and more specific. The star will shine in the sky announcing the birth of the Buddha, for the Buddha is going to be born at dawn this time. And he's going to be born from the knothole of a tree when the first rays of sunlight fall upon it from the sunrise. I'm overcome with joy and anticipation, because I've waited a thousand years for my beloved companion to be born.

The first rays of the sun come. They touch the top of the tree first, descending it as the sun rises (something they wouldn't do in real life). As the rays of the sun touch the knothole, an enormous snake comes out. The snake is huge, a hundred feet long, and he comes straight at me!

I'm so terrified that I fall over backward. Then I get to my feet and run with all the strength that I have. When I think I've gone far enough I look around, only to find that the snake is running in back of me and keeping his flattened head exactly over my head!

So I run twice as hard in terror. But when I turn around and look, there's the snake's head—still exactly over my head! I run still harder and look and the snake is still there, and I know there's no hope. Then, by some intuition, I make a circle by touching my right hip with my right arm. I'm still running, and the snake pokes what he can of his head through the circle and I know the danger is over.

When the dream ends we are still running through the forest, but now the snake and I are talking and the danger has diminished.

This is a very difficult dream to assimilate, especially for a twenty-five-year-old. Such dreams are worthy of a later stage in life, and it is difficult when such a dream comes so early.

What is the snake? The first tumultuous appearance of my fourth, inferior function, a primitive Dionysian quality. Its appearance was certainly too early in a Westerner's life for anybody, let alone me, to cope with. It was many years before I could stand to face the direct impact of it.

I quarreled with my analyst at the time. She said, "You shouldn't dream dreams like that." She meant, of course, that the appearance of the inferior function should never happen to anyone under the age of thirty-five. I replied indignantly, "You don't tell a sixteen-year-old girl that she shouldn't have gotten pregnant. That doesn't help after the fact. If it happened, it happened. One has to cope with it."

For me, the Dionysian quality became insistent, demanding, and virtually unassimilable—a six-foot-two individual and a hundred-foot snake don't make a very good pair. I did indeed lead a driven life, as the end of the dream foretold. For many, many years I was running scared. As Dr. Jung once said, "If you have an assimilating match with a tiger, you know who's going to assimilate whom." The best one can do is make a truce. And the secret for that in this dream was to make a circle. I made a circle with my arm—a mandala to contain the snake. That was form enough. I didn't assimilate the snake, and the snake didn't assimilate me. But we could function; we could go through the woods together.

When Dr. Jung heard of this dream, he lectured me within an inch of my life about its content. He told me that I must live in such and such a way, and that I may trust certain things but to stay away from other things, and so forth. And all from the information contained in that dream. I took the dream to mean I must live in a circle—protected, contained, formed, structured, and very much alone. And that is what I did.

Thirty-five years later, at the much riper age of sixty, the second dream on the subject came up. Thirty-five years is a long time to be patient. During that time I worked very hard on the first dream. I took every word of it and put it through the four steps described on page 75. It was only at age fifty-five that I read a reference to the life of the Buddha which explained one aspect of the dream that had always puzzled me.

It seems that on the night when the Buddha was enlightened, there was a terrible storm. All the dark forces came to put out the light, which was beginnning to glow within the Buddha. And they stormed and they stormed. And Naga, the great world cobra, came and stretched his hood over the Buddha's head to protect him. It dawned on me with a rush of understanding that the snake in my dream had been protecting me, not trying to harm me, and in fact it was not dangerous to me. My enmity and all my running had just made it more difficult for the snake to keep his hood of protection over my head. I felt very foolish.

Here's the second dream:

I'm on a California beach with a family of friends. The woman of the household is a particularly good friend of mine, a very wise woman. She and I are a little distance apart from the family picnic. We are discussing this holiday crush of people on the beach—everybody in the world is there. I can see at least a million people. I like this. I enjoy beaches and good fun and good atmosphere—the happiness, the sun, the children, the picnics, the sports.

But there is one discordant note. The city fathers have brought up a number of old kitchen ranges—wood, gas, electric—and distributed them along the beach, unconnected, so that they don't function at all, except as funky art. Our party has taken up possession of one of these stoves which never produce any heat. They are there only for decoration.

My friend and I discuss the American liking for funky, emotionally shocking things as decorative. We agree that we don't like it. Nonetheless, our picnic party is around one of these stoves.

Suddenly I look up, and who do I see but my snake! He is wriggling around through the crowd and no one but my friend and I see him. He slithers along, making no trouble at all. He comes to a pair of upright posts with a cross-piece at the top and wriggles up and does his thing. He loops and twines, and he goes over himself and back again. I watch him very carefully, because I don't want the snake to find me.

He comes down and begins to wriggle away, and I see that he's moving away from me. I whisper to my friend, "Good, he's going away." But the snake hears this, changes his path, and comes straight for me. I say, "Wouldn't you know it! A million people and he comes straight to me!"

I don't want him to come. I wish he would go away. But for some reason I'm not terrified, and I don't run away as I did before. The snake comes directly at me. At this point there's a break in the dream. There is some work of confrontation, but it's just as if a piece of film had been cut out and the ends spliced back together.

When the dream picks up again the woman is gone and the snake is gone, but a radiant man from heaven—a young fellow who glows— is standing with me. We're friends and we're having a marvelous time. Again, finally, I have my companion.

We walk along and I say, "I didn't realize we were in India." I look again and see that we're not in India—it's just that these blond Americans look so dark compared with the radiant man from heaven that I thought I was among very dark-skinned people. But it was only the contrast, and we were indeed on the beach in Southern California. And I'm so happy. I say to him, "I know this is extraordinary, but I'm as happy as a mortal could be."

We walk on, looking at this and that. He takes me some distance and we come to a dam. The dammed-up river is immensely wide but not very deep. The man from heaven turns to me and says, "All right. The dam is built, the water is backed up. Now you design and build a hydroelectric system for it, and it will fill the energy deficit for the whole world."

That is the evolution of the Dionysian quality, which has occupied most of a lifetime and is by no means complete. Let's take a look at how the Dionysian quality shows its evolution in these two dreams.

The funky stoves, which seemed so strange and inappropriate, had a powerful effect on me. I tend to spend a great deal of time alone. The dream is saying that it's on a public beach, in the most extraverted of Southern California situations, that the snake comes to find me. It's in the middle of funky Southern California, which I tend to disdain, that the enlightenment comes. That's a bitter pill for me, because all my instincts tell me to go to a monastery in the desert to do that last stage of inner work. But the dream informs me that it must be done in the difficult circumstances of a public beach. That was a very large joke on me, but it could be done no other way.

The woman represents the feminine side of me, my *anima*, which is essential in making that deep confrontation with the archetypal world, the inferior function. Jung defined the anima or animus as that organ in one s psyche which mediates between one's conscious personality and the collective unconscious. The woman helped mediate the snake for me simply by being there.

The snake, the primitive Dionysian quality of which I was so frightened, was the god in his more terrifying form. It had me on the run for years, and turned out to be protecting me until I could come to terms with him on the beach, when it was time for a confrontation. (Theoretically, the ego never assimilates an archetype. The best one can do—and all that is required—is to make a mutually reciprocal relationship. If one tries to assimilate an archetype one is likely to be assimilated by it.)

I was still resisting, although I was no longer terrified, so the snake was able to come back to me. I was then able to accept my inferior function and return to the fourth Buddha (which had been in his snakelike, godlike, form). I was ready for the snake's companionship, but with a new perspective: I was now ready to receive the Dionysian energy—the dam—which was there, waiting for me to put into form, and use for the benefit of, more than my own personal life.

13. Ritual and Ceremony: Bringing Joy Home

> I possess God as tranquilly in the bustle of my kitchen . . . as if I were on my knees before the Blessed Sacrament . . . It is not necessary to have great things to do. I turn my little omelet in the pan for the love of God . . . When I cannot do anything else, it is enough for me to have lifted a straw from the earth for the love of God.
>
> BROTHER LAWRENCE

Once you have met the ecstatic archetype through active imagination or dreamwork, you can enrich your experience by bringing the joy you find there into your conscious life. Ritual and ceremony are excellent forms for this. Like an empty cup, you can fill a ritual with joy and drink from it.

We will first explore the nature of ritual, and then see how we can incorporate it into daily life.

The Nature of Ritual

It seems to me that we have two duties in life: We must be responsible members of the culture we are born into, and we must also be everything we are within our deepest selves. To find our way between society's expectations and our spiritual needs is the way of ritual. It is the way that makes the impossible possible.

Ceremony, from a Latin word meaning "sacredness," is an ancient and powerful way to make concrete what you have learned through active imagination and dreamwork. As the poet William Butler Yeats said, "How but in custom and ceremony can innocence and beauty be born?" I would add,

Where else but in ritual and ceremony can those 100,000 volts of divine energy be contained?

Meaningful ritual and ceremony affirm our relationship to the sacred and nourish both the spiritual and secular worlds. Our inner nature needs acknowledgment from our conscious personality as much as our egos need to remember their source in the collective unconscious.

The Lack of Meaningful Ritual in Western Society

We live in an age almost devoid of good-quality ceremony. If one is fortunate enough to be nourished by the great wealth of traditional rituals and ceremonies which are our cultural heritage, one can live safely in this richness. But an increasing number of people lose contact with these old ways and live in psychological poverty. Probably it is a painful but necessary stage of evolution to be denied the nourishment of tradition and collective ritual, but it seems a hallmark of contemporary people that we must address our inner lives as an individual matter. To do this successfully is to come out the other side into a sense of belonging and of community, the Heavenly Jerusalem. But there is a dry, arid time in between the old ways, which are so rich, and the new vision, which is the promise of a new age. It is that arid time which is the concern of any truly contemporary person. The *Bhagavad-Gita* expresses our dilemma: "The world is imprisoned in its own activity except when actions are performed as worship of God."

The point of ritual is not to make magic, to dominate someone or something and make it bend to our will, but to make a divine connection, to experience a momentary unity of the two worlds. Greek artists often portrayed Dionysus and his followers with their heads thrown back in the ecstatic pose, and engaged in their favorite pastime, swinging. Swinging is the symbol of being poised between two worlds. This transcendence is the hallmark of Dionysus, and this is what the

Dionysian ritual aims for. Nicos Kazantzakis put this beautifully in *Report to Greco:*

> Greek serenity is intricate and tragic. A balance between fierce, opposing forces which, after a toilsome and prolonged struggle, succeeded in making peace with each other and in reaching the point prescribed by a Byzantine, mystic effortlessness. In other words, effort's peak.

No drunkenness was permitted in the ancient Dionysian revels, because one had to be aware and conscious to avoid the evil spirits that came along with the aroma of the wine. The worshipers sipped the wine in full consciousness that the wine was the god; and in taking the wine into their bodies they took the divine ecstasy into their spirits.

Today, however, we have forgotten all this. Our models are no longer gods but technology. We speak of "man as machine" and "cybernetic models for thinking," even "artificial intelligence." These images have turned us away from the irrational realm and left us with only our rationality. Half of our potential reality is unlived.

A few of the old Dionysian rituals have survived in America, but usually more as quaint relics and excuses for parties than anything else. Halloween, for example, is a remnant of an old Dionysian ritual. The church rationalizes it by saying that it was the last fling of the evil element before the following day, All Saint's Day, when the souls of the faithful are honored, revered, and respected. But the earlier meaning of Halloween, All Hallow's Evening, was to honor the ecstatic, the Dionysian, even the demonic element of life back-to-back with All Saint's Day. This balancing act made the "good" possible because what was labeled "bad" was also honored.

The same is true of Mardi Gras. In French, *mardi gras* means "fat Tuesday"—the Tuesday before the beginning of Lent, Ash Wednesday. The joyous, ecstatic, Dionysian element of life is honored so that Ash Wednesday, which is a day of penance, austerity, and fasting, might have its own validity. Up until the twelfth century even the monks were allowed out of their monasteries on Mardi Gras. As long as they arrived home by first mass on Ash Wednesday, no questions were asked.

We have not completely excluded Dionysus from religion in our time. We see some return of Dionysus in the charismatic religious groups of all faiths that have arisen in the past few decades. The Quakers, whom we think of as staid, are in fact a remnant in our society of a Dionysian organization. The early group was called Quakers because the members, in their religious ecstasy—a central part of their worship—would quake. The body would begin to tremble and they would be filled with the spirit.

In New England a group called the Shakers persisted well into living memory, into the 1930s. In fact, in early 1987 two members were still alive. We remember them primarily for their furniture—fine, simple, handcrafted work of enduring beauty and strength that reflected their profound belief in God. In fact, the Shakers were another expression of Dionysus. It was a kind of monastic organization of both men and women, who lived separately and never married. As their religious ceremony they would dance at night in what was called a round dance. The men circled clockwise and the women circled counterclockwise until they danced themselves into a religious fervor, shaking and trembling; hence the name Shakers.

In these modern rituals Dionysus lives on. It is not necessary to designate a "Dionysian cult" in which goats are torn apart in order to honor ecstatic expression. The traditions that have come down to us were right and meaningful for the cultures they originally served, for people who believed without reservation in the literal reality of angels and the divine right of kings. But the very fact that we feel uncomfortable with some of these images and beliefs means that we need to search for a contemporary container for them, which is as valid for us as the early ones were for earlier people. In the medieval tradition of the church it was said that the church must change to remain the same. This gives us license to find new ways in order to be loyal to the old.

Creating Our Own Rituals

An old Jewish story, which touches me deeply, illustrates the fact that we do not have to depend on existing structure to make powerful ritual expressions:

Once upon a time there was a great traditional ritual for the inner protection and nourishment of the people. The rabbi and all the people of the community went to a particular tree, in a particular forest, in a particular place, on a particular day, and performed a highly prescribed ritual. Then, so the story goes, there were terrible times. A whole generation was scattered and the ritual was forgotten.

When things got better again, someone remembered that there was an old ritual for protection and nourishment, but he could remember only its overall structure. The rabbi and the people went into the forest, but they'd forgotten exactly which tree was the right tree. So they chose a tree and performed the ritual as best they could. And it was sufficient.

More hard times came, and another generation was excluded from the ritual. Somebody remembered that in the old days their ancestors had gone into the forest and done something, so the rabbi and the people went out into the forest and made up a ritual. And it was sufficient.

And then there were more bad times, and much more was lost. The people remembered that in the good old days their ancestors had done something or other, but they didn't know when or what or where. So they just went out and did the best they could. And it was sufficient.

And then there were more hard times, and all that was left was the vague memory that in the olden days somebody had done something. So the new generation went out and improvised and did the best they could, intending their new ritual to be for the protection and nourishment of the people. And it was sufficient.

The moral to this story is clear: No matter what you do, whether you do it "right" or "wrong," it will be sufficient as long as you do it with consciousness and in the best way that you know how. That is the nature of ritual.

Art as Ritual

We have defined *sensuous* as "the life of the spirit as seen through the senses." This is the world of artists and poets, and this is the world of Dionysus, whose teachers were the Muses. Through works of art we can glimpse the spirit.

Through the arts, as with ritual and ceremony, we can live out those parts of ourselves that can have no practical expression. In this sense both art and ritual are, paradoxically, ways of doing something but not doing it. We satisfy the inner urge without doing external damage.

Our culture and the values we get from it demand that we give up in outer form the rougher Dionysian element. Thus for modern people so much of the Dionysian element is to be found in subtle forms of art, or ritual, or ceremony. Our disciplined Western faculties will go dead, dry, and colorless unless some Dionysian elements are included in them. Very often these "spectator sports"—looking at paintings, listening to music, watching movies, and so on—are the only way for us to get this refined Dionysian expression—and thank God for them!

The arts have always been a source of ritual for humankind, a way to express the inexpressible. In fact it is only in comparatively recent times that we have separated "art" from the rest of human expression. Many ancient cultures had real spiritual unity. What we have come to think of as their art—decorative pottery, sculpture, votive objects, paintings, dwellings, even weapons—were an extension and expression of the spiritual dimension, which they accepted without question as an integral part of life.

Theater and religious expression are closely related. We have seen how the celebration of Dionysus led to the creation of classical Greek theater. Similarly, the Mystery plays of Jesus led to Western theater. The word "profane," which we think of as blasphemy, originally meant "porch of the church." When dramas were a highly introverted expression they were done inside the church, near the altar: That was the worship of God. When a play or drama or ritual was made for the populace it was done on the porch of the church, and expressed outward for the mass of people to see. Polish director Jerzy Grotowski has said,

The theater, when it was still part of religion, was already theater: it liberated the spiritual energy of the congregation or tribe by incorporating myth and profaning or rather transcending it. The spectator thus had a renewed awareness of his personal truth in the truth of the myth, and through fright and a sense of the sacred he came to catharsis.

George Bernard Shaw once said that "fine art is the only teacher except torture." I would add that those things which turn up in our lives as symptoms—certainly a form of torture—can be expressed ritually in arts such as painting, sculpture, poetry, novels, plays, films.

One of the great Dionysian flows in our culture is the call of the South Sea islands. Almost everybody in our technological culture has South Sea Islands fantasies, and they are most emphatically Dionysian in nature. The paintings of Paul Gaugin, a French painter at the turn of the century, express and embody for others the Dionysian dimension in which the artist was caught up.

For some years Gaugin, a successful stockbroker, had been a frustrated Sunday painter. One day he threw over his job and family and literally went off to the South Seas, where he painted scores of sensuous, colorful paintings of voluptuous island women that are considered masterpieces of modern art.

Gaugin went to the South Seas in search of a paradise, but he found instead a personal hell. His own life was a miserable mess and he died of syphilis in Tahiti. But—and this is the important part—he *painted* a paradise; and by means of his art, his ritual, he found the paradise he was looking for. And when we look at his paintings we too get some of this Dionysian quality and are refreshed.

Making Our Own Dionysian Rituals

Now that we have learned something of the transformative nature of ritual, we shall see how we can incorporate ritual—and Dionysian ritual in particular—into our own lives, making them richer and more deeply lived in the process.

Basic Rules

Before you engage in any ritual activities, please read and remember the following basic rules. (If you wish more detailed information on creating and ritualizing experiences, please see *Inner Work*.)

1. *Don't do anything that would hurt others,* literally or on the unconscious level. When you perform rituals you unleash powerful psychological energy, and it is most rewarding to aim this energy toward a good and constructive purpose.
2. *Have respect and courtesy for others and for yourself.*
3. *Don't provoke confrontation or be dramatic.* This is not good use of ritual and its nature is inflation, not enthusiasm. It will not achieve any productive result.
4. *Affirm your personal responsibility for the Dionysian quality.* Dionysian ecstasy is yours to channel, to humanize. Use it to produce positive, enlivening energy.

Getting Started

Getting started with ritual is very difficult for many of us. Ritual is so seldom included in our daily lives that when we find ourselves involved in a ceremony—even a familiar one such as a wedding—we may begin to feel embarrassed. This is especially true when the ritual we are performing is of our own creation. It is easy to think that the whole idea of ritual is silly and that nothing real can come of it. But ceremony and its results are very real. Don Quixote once commented that he was searching for the bread that was "better than wheat"—a reference to the Host. Ceremony in its depth is "realer than real," just as the Host is more real than wheat.

Ceremony is a conscious event. Even the smallest act can become a powerful ritual. An act performed with symbolic intent sets up an exchange between the unconscious and the conscious that allows for progression toward unity. This exchange can move in two directions: A consciously performed act will effect deep psychological change. A ritual act that springs from a change in unconscious attitude will be expressed as a change in conscious attitude.

Psychologically, ritual is symbolic behavior. Please do not think that you have to engage in wild midnight revels to create a Dionysian ritual; you do not. Jung cautioned that,

The pagan religions met this danger by giving drunken ecstasy a place within their cult. Heraclitus doubtless saw what was at the back of it when he said, "But Hades is the same Dionysos in whose honour they go mad and keep the feast of the wine-vat." For this very reason orgies were granted religious license, so as to exorcise the danger that threatened from Hades. Our solution, however, has served to throw the gates of hell wide open.

I am in a terrible dilemma because, although I stoutly respect and advocate public ceremonies, I can't stand to do many of these things myself! I suspect that many people are like me. We learn to make rituals with our own personal expression. Of course, if you are fortunate enough to be comfortable with the old ways or with some of the new, modern, collective experiences, this would be an excellent way for you to express the ecstatic dimension.

Personalizing Rituals:
Using Conscious Intent To Effect Deep Change

We modern people have to tailor our rituals for the exact situation we are in. For example, perhaps you would like to express something that is not possible to express directly—deep love for your best friend's spouse, for example. This can have no outer manifestation, because it would be destructive on a number of levels. You might ritualize your expression of love, however, by giving a gift to that person; or, if even this is impossible, to someone you designate as a symbol in his or her place. If you invest the gift with your love, then in giving this symbol you will have ritually expressed your love. You would be surprised at how much lighter you can feel after even such a small ceremony!

Ritual can relieve us of something that has become an obsession and which is doing us absolutely no good at all. I knew a man who desperately wanted to run a four-minute mile but simply couldn't accomplish it. The harder he tried the worse it got, and he even found himself going slower because of it. The unattainable mile had become his enemy, and it began to seem that the more he ran the further away it was. Running had become a grueling chore completely devoid of pleasure.

I suggested to him that instead of being angry at the mile, he honor it with the simple gesture of walking around the block. Holding the image of the four-minute mile in his mind, feeling himself in fact having run the distance, he walked in great consciousness around the block. Afterward he found he had let his obsession go, and on a deep level had accomplished his goal. Later, with renewed intent and with much less effort, he was indeed able to run well and joyously.

Running—indeed, all sports—are natural Dionysian activities. We have all heard of the runner's high, that rush of euphoria that floods through runners after they have gone past their personal "wall." This is a wonderful way to call up the joyous Dionysian energy. Those of us who cannot personally take part in a sport can reap some benefit by watching others participate. Football and baseball games certainly release a great deal of suppressed Dionysian energy, and the Olympics—which have been watched on television by something like 40 percent of the world's population—are great unifying forces. If you can participate in sports with some consciousness of their ritual aspect, you can make psychological as well as physical leaps!

Rituals can also be used as a source of spiritual refreshment. One day before a lecture I became so caught up in worrying about what I was going to say that I had no energy for the lecture itself. A wise woman friend who was with me that day gave me excellent advice as to how I could call up the Dionysian energy that I sorely needed. She told me to roll a heavy towel into a ball and throw it on the floor with all the force I could muster, and to do this consciously in honor of Dionysus. Five minutes with that towel put a light in my eye and a spark in the lecture.

Ritualizing Unconscious Images: Changing Behavior with Images from Dreams or Active Imagination

Now that we have seen how we can use conscious intent to effect change on the unconscious level, let's see how we can create rituals based on unconscious material to effect positive behavioral change. The images for these rituals may come through active imagination or dreamwork.

Active Imagination

Remember the woman who was told to express Dionysus by jumping up and down, hands held above her head, shouting as loudly as she could? This is an example of a ritual that appears spontaneously during active imagination. Such rituals spring from the unconscious, and often surprise us with their power and energy. Our archetypal images understand ritual to a far greater degree than our conscious minds ever can. Therefore we can confidently ask these images to give us appropriate ceremonies.

Dreams

We can also get ritual actions from our dreams. By performing concrete actions based on symbolic dream images we can find ourselves suddenly able to comprehend these often puzzling archetypal messages. The following story is about a woman who first ritualized her dream image unconsciously, and later learned to do it consciously so that it provided her with a deep understanding of Dionysian expression.

This woman had been working very hard on her dreams, and she read somewhere that a good way to feel more freedom in waking life was to teach yourself to fly in your dreams. Flying is symbolic of soaring free, and flying in dreams can be very exhilarating.

So every night she went to sleep telling herself, "Tonight I will learn to fly." And every night in her dreams she would find herself on an open plain, ready to fly, but she couldn't seem to get off the ground. She would jump into the air and flap her arms, but nothing would happen. Finally, she found that the only way she could make any progress was to make swimming motions with her arms. In this way she got up off the ground and was able to fly in a rudimentary way. It wasn't exactly the soaring of the spirit she had in mind, but it was the best she could do.

One day a friend convinced her that swimming, which she had never particularly liked, would be a wonderful form of exercise. For weeks it was all she could do to get across the pool and back. But one day she found herself swimming effortlessly. He dream image came flooding back into her mind and the swimming and flying seemed to merge, filling her with an overwhelming feeling of joy.

Through the dream her unconscious self had communicated to her ego the message that swimming would be the wav for her to achieve spiritual release. Even though she began swimming without any conscious intent, she did in fact concretize the dream image. She now approaches her swimming with conscious awareness of its connection to the Dionysian experience, and it has taken on an added dimension. For her, swimming has become a bridge between the two worlds.

Ritualizing the Family Fight

Let's take a look at what we can do to ritualize family fights. By putting an end to these anima–animus tugs-of-war we can do much to reunite the divine androgyne and bring ourselves closer to the self-nurturing Dionysian ideal.

I once knew a young couple who were good people and filled with energy, but troubled. The fellow came to me one day and said, "I'm at the end of my rope. Every weekend my wife and I have the most vicious fights. We start on Saturday morning and we fight and fight, screaming at each other and saying terrible things. By late Sunday afternoon, like clockwork, she starts throwing dishes and I storm out—because I know that if I stay, I'm going to beat her up.

"I'm so guilty and I don't know what to do. It's barbaric. I don't want to live like this and neither does she. But we can't seem to stop ourselves."

To me, their fight seemed to have all the elements of a ritual, but not a very constructive one! So I said, "Why not try having a ritual fight on Saturday morning and see what happens?" He gave me a skeptical look, but agreed to try.

So, the following Saturday morning, feeling awkward but determined to end their fighting, they began their ritual. They stood in the center of the bedroom and bowed to each other, much as opponents in a judo match would do. They exchanged their opinions under the strictest, most formal rules of courtesy and respect. They were free to say whatever they wished as long as they followed this rule. When each felt that there was no more to say, they again stood in the center of the room, bowed to each other, and formally closed the exchange. In this way the fight was symbolically confined within the circle of the ceremony and would not leak into everyday life.

The husband came back to me later and said, "It's the darndest thing. I don't understand it, but it works. Saturday morning, early, we got up and had the ritual fight and enjoyed an idyllic weekend."

I replied, "You have discovered ritual. You paid tribute to the god, and the rest of the weekend was yours. You have taken the Dionysian element in its crudest, roughest, least intelligent form and discovered the stuff of miracle, its transformation into ecstasy and joy."

Epilogue

What is joy?

We can say, as the dictionary does, that it is "an exultation of the spirit, the beatitude of paradise." We can say that, unlike the ephemeral state of happiness, it is a lasting value that nourishes and sustains the spirit as well as the body. Joy does not induce a craving for more, because it is enough.

However, we cannot say what joy is. We must go the further step and discover its true nature for ourselves. When we can make peace with the Dionysian element we will begin to see the glow of ecstasy that enlivens every living thing. And, in the fiery glow of ecstasy, joy can be born within us.

Notes

THE WORLDS OF PSYCHOLOGY AND MYTH

ix "The multiplicity of . . . " C. G. Jung, Sermo IV, from *Memories, Dreams and Reflections* (New York: Random House, 1963).

xiii "For indeed our . . . " Anthony Storr, *The Essential Jung* (Princeton, N.J.: Princeton University Press, 1983), 417.

I. ECSTASY: UNDERSTANDING THE PSYCHOLOGY OF JOY

4 "The characteristic of . . . " Monica Sjöö and Barbara Mor, *The Great Cosmic Mother* (San Francisco: Harper & Row, 1987), 235.

2. WHAT IS ECSTASY?

11 "Ecstasy's not the . . . " Joan Didion, *Slouching Towards Bethlehem* (New York: Dell, 1968), 120.

11 "the *dancing universe* . . . " Fritjof Capra, *The Tao of Physics* (Boulder, Col.: Shambhala Publications, 1975), 276.

3. THE RISE AND FALL OF DIONYSUS

15 "Man is concerned . . . " Ezra Pound, quoted in Lawrence Russ, "The Whole and the Flowing," *Parabola*, vol. VIII, no. 3 (August 1983): 83.

4. THE OTHER SIDE OF ECSTASY

18 "what would it . . . " Marie Louise von Franz, *The Psychological Meaning of Redemption Motifs in Fairy Tales* (Toronto, Canada: Inner City Books, n.d.), 4.

19 "The gigantic catastrophes . . . " C. G. Jung, *Psychological Reflections*, edited and compiled by Jolande Jacobi (Princeton, N.J.: Princeton University Press, 1953).

5. CELEBRATION OF ECSTASY

28 "From joy springs . . . " Ajit Mookerjee, *Ritual Art of India* (New York: Thames and Hudson, 1985.)

6. WOMEN AND DIONYSUS: CELEBRATION OF LIFE

34 "Anthropologist Jacquetta Hawkes . . . " Monica Sjöö and Barbara Mor, *The Great Cosmic Mother* (San Francisco: Harper & Row, 1987), 121.

7. ANDROGYNY: THE UNION OF MALE AND FEMALE

37 "The anima and . . . " Anthony Storr, *The Essential Jung* (Princeton, N.J.: Princeton University Press, 1983), 415.

10. THE GOD CONNECTION

53 "You do not have . . . " From a private conversation between Robert Johnson and Carl Jung.

54 "The essential function . . . " C. G. Jung, from *Psychological Types*, quoted in Anthony Storr, *The Essential Jung* (Princeton, N.J.: Princeton University Press, 1983), 144–145.

11. ACTIVE IMAGINATION: MEETING THE ARCHETYPE

66 "In this way . . . " Anthony Storr, *The Essential Jung* (Princeton, N.J.: Princeton University Press, 1983), 116.

12. DREAMWORK: WORKING WITH THE ARCHETYPE

74 "How often does . . . " Jolande Jacobi, ed., *Paracelsus: Selected Writings*, translated by Norbert Gutterman. Bollingen Series 28 (Princeton, N.J.: Princeton University Press, 1979), 134–136.

13. RITUAL AND CEREMONY: BRINGING JOY HOME

82 "I possess God . . . " From *The Practice of the Presence of God*, by Brother Lawrence of the Resurrection, translated by Sister Mary David. Quoted in *Parabola*, vol. VIII, no. 3 (August 1982): 54.

84 "Greek serenity is . . . " Nicos Kazantzakis, *Report to Greco* (New York: Simon and Schuster, 1965), 154.

88 "The theatre, when . . . " Jerzy Grotowski, *Towards a Poor Theatre* (New York: Simon and Schuster, 1968), 22–23.

90 "The pagan religions . . . " C. G. Jung, *Collected Works*, Bollingen series 12 (Princeton, N.J.: Princeton University Press) 143.